# GALAXIES ON THE GROUND

# GALAXIES ON THE GROUND

2016–2017 WITS Student Anthology

Writers in the Schools (WITS) is a youth program of Literary Arts, a community-based nonprofit literary organization centered in Portland, Oregon, whose mission is to support writers, engage readers, and inspire the next generation with great literature.

925 SW Washington St.
Portland, OR 97205
www.literary-arts.org

*Galaxies on the Ground*
2016-2017 WITS Student Anthology





**Anthology Staff**
Editor: Mel Wells
Designers: AHA (cover)
Mel Wells (interior)

Published by Literary Arts, a 501(c)(3) in Portland, OR

First Edition 2017

Printed in the USA

# 2016-17 WITS Community

WRITERS-IN-RESIDENCE

Turiya Autry, Alex Behr, Cooper Lee Bombardier, Arthur Bradford, Leslee Chan, David Ciminello, Lisa Eisenberg, James Gendron, Courtenay Hameister, Jamie Houghton, Emiko Jean, Brian Kettler, Ramiza Koya, Kathleen Lane, Bettina de León Barrera, Zeloszelos Marchandt, Monty Mickelson, Amy Minato, Laura Moulton, Mark Pomeroy, Matthew Robinson, Joanna Rose, Stacey Tran

VISITING AUTHORS

P.C. Cast, Matthew Desmond, Ed Edmo, Louise Erdrich, Michael Lewis, Colum McCann, Tracy K. Smith

PARTICIPATING TEACHERS

Zandra Ah Choy-Agusen, Scott Blevins, Susie Brighouse, Deanna Delgado, Amanda-Jane Elliot, Kelly Gomes, Ben Grosscup, Jordan Gutlerner, Crystal Hanson, Henry Hooper, Jamie Incorvia, Doug Jenkins, Anne Meadows, Dave Mylet, Jennifer Newton, Mike Nolan, Courtney Palmer, Nathan Pier, Cesar Ramirez, Tina Roberts, Tory Rodgers, Clair Roix, Norman Stremming, Shawn Swanson, Amy Taramasso, Trisha Todd, Dana Vinger, Kim Wagner, Kristin Wallace Knight, Crystel Weber, Alethea Work

PARTICIPATING PRINCIPALS

Petra Callin, Carol Campbell, Peyton Chapman, Brian Chatard, Lorna Fast Buffalo Horse, Ayesha Freeman, Filip Hristic, John Koch, Molly Ouche, Juanita Valder, Curtis Wilson

# CONTENTS

# Introduction

Dear Reader,

At Literary Arts, our mission is to engage readers, support writers, and inspire the next generation with great literature. These goals are exemplified in the work we do with young people. Our programs for high school age students include Writers in the Schools, Verselandia, Students to the Schnitz, and the College Essay Mentoring Project.

Writers in the Schools is the heart of Youth Programs at Literary Arts, offering students opportunities to write, publish, and perform their own creative work. In 2016-2017, 23 brilliant professional writers in multiple genres—including poetry, fiction, creative nonfiction, comics, and playwriting—joined high school classes as artists in residence. Student participants explored multiple genres, learned the habits of a writer, and experienced firsthand how creative expression serves as a catalyst for self-knowledge and increased engagement in their schools and communities.

The anthology you hold in your hands, *Galaxies on the Ground*, evokes the many worlds that coexist in our local high schools. This year's student writing reflects the battlegrounds and shifts in our culture alongside more internal dilemmas; there are stories of young love and academic struggle, as well as insightful commentary on social issues such as racism, immigration, and LGBTQ rights. The hearts and minds of Portland's youth are here, on the page, unfiltered and honest.

Thanks to all who helped make this book. Our interns, Alexandria Baker and Kate Jayroe, both came from Portland State University. As always, thanks to AHA creative agency for the beautiful cover. And special thanks to Mel Wells, Associate Manager of Programs at Literary Arts, for her hard work as editor and designer. This anthology's success is because of her.

Thank you to all of our supporters, including the 31 educators—principals, teachers, and librarians—at the 11 high schools we worked in, and the many individuals and organizations who contributed to our programs: it is because of you that these transformative residencies are possible.

This was a year when it felt like our work together mattered more than ever. Thank you for reading.

Ramiza Koya
*Director of Youth Programs*

## Water {A Collective Poem}

The Students in Room 134
WILSON HIGH SCHOOL
WITS WRITER: BETTINA DE LEÓN BARRERA

As the memories poured out into stories
The snowflakes create patterns like galaxies on the ground
Fir trees of green and white-capped waves
Moving along a blue water artery
Thing is a normal color
There are no bodies, just a sea of ever-editing souls
The side that hides from the sun

## Sequence

*Recipient of the Oregonian/OregonLive Prize for Nonfiction*

Ilse Stacklie-Vogt
FRANKLIN HIGH SCHOOL
WITS WRITER: LESLEE CHAN

-The Old House-

Tender soil is working its way into the soft rolls of my infant legs, unmarred but for where diaper rash has ravaged. The CD cover is pale blue; I hang on to little tomatoes as my father sings to me.

-The Mountains-

Still in the age of CDs, Dad requests B-52s. We are beachward bound, dancing to "Love Shack" with flailing childhood spirit. Whizzing along a road that winds up anticipation of blue horizons.

-San Francisco-

The fetid haze of teenage stench that hangs about the van is disregarded. These eight girls are on a high. "Shut Up and Dance" blasts in humid gusts as we make our heroic return to hotel rooms of leftover fries from BJ's.

-The Lodge-

Uncle Jim abandons Air Force precision. We swerve past icicles that are dragon's teeth and scream "When We Were Young" so loudly that Adele is nowhere to be heard, Fireball a warm weight in our gut.

-Camp Namanu-

Campers permanently dirt-stained from adventures by horseback and sleeping in meadows crowd the wobbly benches as Thumper thumps out some Death Cab for Cutie on his guitar. We follow each other into the darkness of our cabins, brimming with the kind of tears that come from having too much love for smoke in your eyes.

-The Hot Tub-

Life lit up soft pink under the stars. For the length of a song, we let Jack Johnson's "Upside Down" speak for us. Rain carpets the golf course to our left and we run out barefoot and barely clothed. It is cold.

-Leaving Sun River-

Sunday Morning rain is falling first on toothbrush trees, then painted canyons. Memories of tangled bodies drip nostalgia as we all drive separate roads home.

-My Soon-to-be Girlfriend's Kitchen-

She lends me her black Poler sweatshirt when we go to the store to get blueberries. Making ebelskivers, I reach around her waist from behind, rather than step to the side. She turns on Jack Johnson while we cook and I take the gentle melody of "Times Like These" to mean *yes, I like you, too.*

-A Snow Day-

She cradles her guitar reluctantly. Lush snowdrifts out the window soften my pestering. Hours pass lazily; we sit so that our legs touch. "Please play me a song," I say. The opening notes of "Dirty Paws" fall in time with the blizzard, rich and warm.

-The Futon-

Kissing to jazz feels like the slow movement of red wine when it's poured. Louis Armstrong sounds like chocolate and slow dancing and soft smiles with closed eyes. She tastes faintly of cold brew and whispered breaths. "'You Go to My Head' is our song," she says.

# The Cell Phone

Issa Mohamed
BENSON HIGH SCHOOL
WITS WRITER: MONTY MICKELSON

Syria used to be a beautiful country. Omar used to live a normal life full of peace, hope, and dreams, until the day when everything changed. It was that day in 2012 when a little boy decided to write on the school's wall "I hate the president. People want to get rid of him." That day ended with a lot of children being arrested. Syrian people started protesting across the country, demanding that the government release them, but the government forces responded by firing on them and killing dozens. Months later civil war began.

The war has many sides such as the Assad regime forces, Free Syrian Army, and ISIS. Each side was looking to control more territory, no matter how many innocent people they would kill. Omar and his family were expecting to die any second. Besides all of this, he was an immigrant.

Omar's life was extra difficult compared to any other boy in the city because of his race, his color, and his hairstyle. Every day he was targeted by police officers, and he began to get used to it. They make fun of his Afro and his color, then they let him go. But one day something unexpected happened to him.

Omar was playing beside his house with his friends, trying to have fun like any other boy. Four police officers came up to him and started questioning him.

EXTERIOR: A STREET IN DAMASCUS, SYRIA – DAY

POLICE OFFICER
Where you from, boy?

OMAR
Somalia. What is wrong?

POLICE OFFICER
So what you doing here? Go back to your country!

OMAR
I was born here and I am also studying here!

POLICE OFFICER
Oh, really? So, do you have a phone?

OMAR
Yes, I do.

POLICE OFFICER
Let me see it. I want to see if you have anything illegal. *(like picture of the Free Syrian Army, or video of the revolution)*

OMAR
OK. *(hands the phone to the police officer, feeling comfortable that he doesn't have anything illegal in it)*

POLICE OFFICER
Wow, nice phone.

OMAR
Yes, I know.

POLICE OFFICER
I have to take your phone with me. I will check it and I will be right back in five minutes.

OMAR
No, you are going nowhere with my phone. I know you will never come back.

POLICE OFFICER
It seems like you want to go to jail. Do you?

OMAR
No, I don't want to, but you won't take my phone.

POLICE OFFICER
*(to his friends)* Get the car. We got to take him with us.

AHMED *(Omar's friend)*
Let him take the damn phone. Your life is worth more than a device. Let him take it.

*(Omar starts looking around, trying to find a way to escape from the four police officers but he cannot find any way to go. The four police officers surround him, waiting for Omar to either say yes and let the phone go or say no and take him with the phone. At the time, people who went to jail didn't survive for more than a couple weeks.*

*The police officer looks at his waist and puts his hand on his gun as a way to tell Omar, "Do not waste my time; I want this phone and I will take it." Omar has no choice except giving the phone away and saving his life.)*

OMAR
*(talks with water in his eyes)* Alright, alright, take the phone but let me and my friend go.

POLICE OFFICER
*(yelling)* Do you think I want your phone because I need money? *(pulls $200 out of his pocket)* See how much I have? Now get the hell out of here.

*(Omar's friend felt happy to be free to go home, but Omar was crying. He cried not because they took his phone but because he could not do anything.)*

OMAR
I'm sure if I was a Syrian boy they would not have done the same to me.

*(Eventually, after many similar actions like that and after about seven months, the International Organization for Migration gave Omar and his family an opportunity to move to the United States. As he moved he had to learn English. It was difficult at the beginning, but by his first year he completed The Portland International School Academy. Then, in his second year he finished his classes with a 3.7 GPA, and in the third year he won an Achievement Award from Club Z. Now he is on track to graduate from Benson High School.)*

## The Cacophony

Micah Von Werssowetz
MADISON HIGH SCHOOL
WITS WRITER: JAMIE HOUGHTON

In so much space it spun and shrieked
Sliding out and sliding in
Synthetic but sore
Saw teeth grinding in imitated grins
Or grimacing at this feeling across the skin it grew
So it branched
Bleached bone and circuits
Limbs of sound and twisting fury
A loom of nerves entwining into a spine
Pining for the first time
And finding pleasure in its anger and its hate
It crawled from the muddy haze it was born in,
All ribs and rust
And clawhammer hands
The Cacophony stood and smiled
Piano wire drawing back purple swollen lips
And heard the breeze break on its glass teeth
Too few and too many at once
As it took a breath of stagnant sweaty air
And gave the world the gift of sound

That day the shores first hummed
And the trees first creaked
The creeks first babbled in broken words
And water boiled for the first time
The Cacophony first stood and sang
And the earth cracked and cackled, its plates all broke
And began to drift
The first day the Cacophony sang,
The breeze came all at once, tearing it up
Splitting it again and again

Bashing it on every rock and giving it to every bird
The Cacophony sang even then
And all it touched learned to sing back
Trees learned to fall
Lightning learned thunder
Like waves learned shores
Like mountains learned fire

That was the day The Cacophony first sang
And gave the world the gift of sound
And was murdered and raped and praised and fucked and worshiped and screamed from every deathbed
And it was so ugly
The way it crashed against the cliffs
And taught them to break
The way it grabbed our lungs and squeezed
And taught us to scream
Until we came undone, into light and flowers and blood
We came undone, into sex and sedatives
We came undone, into blades and cogs
Into wire
Armatures for sound to dress us in our skins and light and hate

That was the day The Cacophony stood
And made us into music.

## Bear's Flowers

*Recipient of the Cosmic Monkey Comics Prize for Comics*

Leanne Rose
LINCOLN HIGH SCHOOL
WITS WRITER: LISA EISENBERG

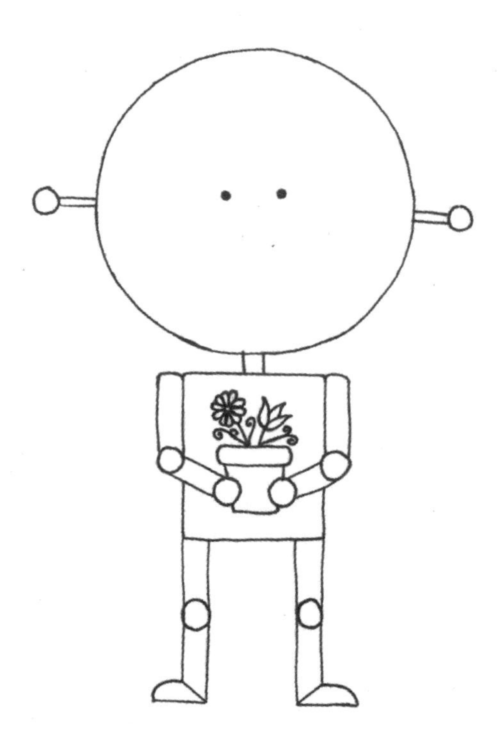

I AM BEAR.

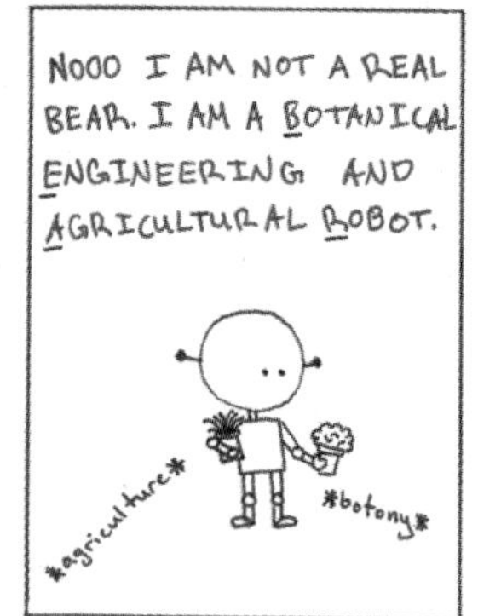
NOOO I AM NOT A REAL BEAR. I AM A BOTANICAL ENGINEERING AND AGRICULTURAL ROBOT.
*agriculture*
*botony*

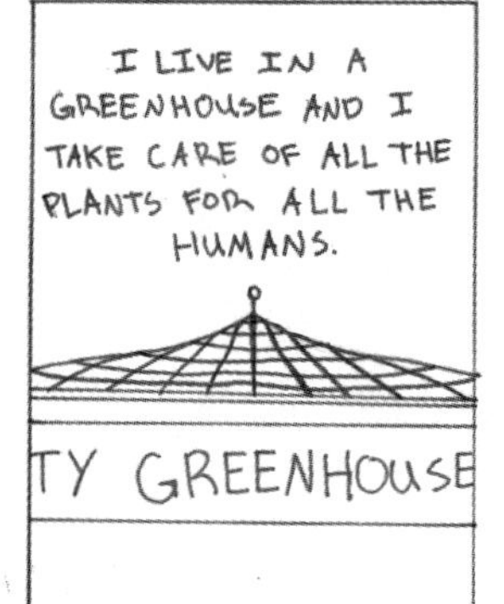
I LIVE IN A GREENHOUSE AND I TAKE CARE OF ALL THE PLANTS FOR ALL THE HUMANS.
TY GREENHOUSE

THESE ARE CARROTS.
THEY ARE... GOOD CARROTS.

AND THESE ARE MY FLOWERS. THEY ARE FRAGILE. BEAR TAKES CARE OF THE FLOWERS.

BEAR HAS NEVER LEFT THE GREENHOUSE. OUTSIDE, HE THINKS THAT...

THERE ARE LOTS OF BIG, GREEN TREES LIKE IN HIS HOME.

BIG TREES...

BEAR ALSO THINKS THERE ARE MANY NICE PEOPLE.
GAYS
GET BACK IN THE KITCHEN!

AND JUST LIKE BEAR PROTECTS HIS GREENHOUSE...

THOSE NICE PEOPLE PROBABLY DO A LOT TO PROTECT THEIR EARTH.

THERE ARE MANY FRAGILE PLANTS IN HERE.

THERE MUST BE SO MANY OUT THERE TO PROTECT.

BEAR WOULD LIKE TO GO OUTSIDE AND SEE HOW NICE HU-

## Mexico

Stephanie Alvarado
PARKROSE HIGH SCHOOL
WITS WRITER: JAMIE HOUGHTON

I loved it there because it made me happy.
I felt so much happiness like at home
with all of the most caring and loving people
that would ask how you are doing.
The pace was calm and dreamy like the best dream anyone can ever have.
The sunshine was brighter than ever
and the stars would light up the night.
When the sunshine was bright we would go fishing to
the muddy river 'til the sun was no longer visible.
I walked through the streets as the sun shined in my dark brown eyes,
And the low wind would blow my thick straight hair.
I remember Abuela's words, "Be very careful."
As I ran outside and played those words
would disappear and fly away like the birds,
I walked on the crooked sidewalks with the cracking concrete.
Abuela would say, "Don't fall."
On our way to the ice cream lady everyone would wave
and say *¿hola cómo estás?*
Their smiles were brighter than the stars that lit up the night.
The ice cream was the best homemade ice cream
I could taste the rich creamy fresh strawberries
in every bite I took.
As Abuelita and I walked back home
I could hear the music that would play for hours and hours
In La Estacion.
I could smell the tacos from miles away
but at the corner of the taco shop I could smell the dirty farm animals
And see the flies flying on them.
Each day flew faster than the flies outside and the sun
would come down faster than ever.
I remember Abuelita's words
"I love you, take care and hope to see you very soon."
Perhaps it won't be very long.

## To be a Bookworm

Sophia Lynsky
ROOSEVELT HIGH SCHOOL
WITS WRITER: JOANNA ROSE

To teleport home from Narnia
is to meet a centaur
and to meet a centaur
is to have your cat as the mayor.
To witness magic
is to be glued to your book
and to look up from your book
is to teleport home from Narnia.

## When the silence was loud, so the memories had to scream

Tiffany Vo
CLEVELAND HIGH SCHOOL
WITS WRITER: COOPER LEE BOMBARDIER

I remember the wind pushing against my face with my adolescent hands tight around the leather jacket, as we drove the motorcycle through the chaotic market streets of Vietnam.
I remember seeing my mother's face for the first time. She told me I came out of the womb slowly and silently—I was their miracle baby.
I remember the cold floor of my pale yellow room.
I remember the grass and the roses that dotted the barbwire fence of our liberty blue house.
I remember the heads with soulless eyes that haunted me in my sleep.
I remember Las Vegas and crying because I thought the fireworks could have fallen on me.
I remember being scared of Batman.
I remember the bathtub of pillows in the kindergarten classroom.
I remember the green milk of Saint Patrick's Day.
I remember never feeling like I belonged anywhere.
I remember falling face-first off the monkey bars.
I remember the second time my family moved, the little red house.
I remember befriending Annie. During recess we would go into the school garden and concoct snakeskin potions and floral leaf tonics.
I remember the rocks, the stars, and the moon that were always there for me.
I remember dreaming of what death would feel like, and how I was scared of falling back into a dark hole of nothing.
I remember the rubber backpack and not understanding who God was; I never believed in religion.
I remember eating ramen noodles on Styrofoam cubes while watching soap operas with my mom.
I remember the snow of 2008 and the best Christmas that came with it.
I remember moving to a castle; it was the third time I had moved.
I remember being told I was bratty when I was younger, but had completely changed after the birth of my younger sister.

I remember seeing a picture of McKenzie's first smile.
I remember changing everything about me to fit in with the other kids.
I remember the sleek and modern school so completely different from the run-down, grimy charm of the others I was used to.
I remember feeling like the library at my new school was a haven. Nothing could go wrong.
I remember the boy who told me my people killed his grandfather.
I remember drawing bobcats and parrots and learning about minerals—the amethyst teacher.
I remember the pool I spent my summers at.
I remember moving again to a small apartment and escaping often to the forest fields nearby. There was a secret treehouse the neighborhood kids would go to. The girls picked bouquets of wildflowers. The boys played pirates. In the evenings, we would all lay under the blanket of indigo and speak more to the stars than to each other about our greatest fears and dreams.
I remember the wedding where I danced in the poof-iest gown and did so without a care in the world.
I remember seeing an old friend in a music class.
I remember moving for the fifth time, an old peachy house that creaked and grumbled, but loved and cherished us. There's a large tree in the front. Its trunk bent low enough to be a hammock.
I remember the willow trees in my life. I love them.
I remember wanting to be invisible, planning to never speak a word in sixth grade.
I remember being frustrated that I was ripped away again from friends I had barely gotten to know.
I remember later in life, as I gave a presentation about myself in a high school classroom that I was okay with the moves, because I reinvented myself every time. I kept the parts of me that aligned with who I was and ditched the parts that made me feel like I was conforming, or someone else.
I remember promising myself to be positive, no matter the situation—to always have hope.
I remember the bumpy 6:00 a.m. bus rides to school, where we doodled in our sketch pads and hummed to The Plain White T's *Rhythm of Love.*

I remember her leaving me for California.
I remember relieving myself of the weight on my shoulders by telling her my deepest secret—I was never who I said I was.
I remember the solar system cake; I ate Saturn.
I remember Swiss and turkey with tomato and lettuce on sourdough.
I remember the hill I rolled down and the ice cream floats after.
I remember meeting new people again.
I remember thinking I knew what true love felt like. I was five.
I remember the rainbow tights, Hanna Andersson dresses and braids.
I remember discovering my favorite song again and again and again and again.
I remember avoiding strawberry cakes because of the fight.
I remember that hospital room where my dying aunt exchanged her last words to me: "Hello."
I remember riding in the front seat and being scared to death he'd crash the car.
I remember the realization of my color, my race, my ancestry, and how I was different from all of them.
I remember wanting to seek justice, to be outraged for them, because I knew that feeling.
I remember the sun greeting me with its warmth, the salty air biting the tips of my body, and the cold water numbing my senses. I was ready to leave and be one with the sea.
I remember my dad's smile that day at the rocks, wholesome and good—that's him.
I remember the blue streaks in their hair.
I remember comparing myself to other girls and figuring out it was no good.
I remember giving orphaned caterpillars homes.
I remember the funeral for the sunflowers Theo, Sarah, and I grew.
I remember calling it colorful language.
I remember the spices, the lanterns that adorned the bamboo houses, and the people who made SuZhou so special.
I remember feeling sorry for myself.
I remember avoiding Harry Potter books because of their scary covers.
I remember the spiral notebooks I kept, filled to the brim with my storyboards of books I had yet to write.

I remember my mom tucking me in, telling me she loves me.
I remember all of the artwork I had given to my friends returned to my cubby box. That was when I knew.
I remember the teacher who gave up her dreams of being a singer because her beloved family had become her new dream.
I remember March 4th, 2016.
I remember the cherry blossom tree that held me and comforted me at my lows.
I remember the sweet jazz of New Orleans that shook my being and awakened me to a world I would come to know and love.
I remember the secret to life. Hint: it's a secret.
I remember
I remember
I remember

## The Final Showdown

Karolina Skupien
LINCOLN HIGH SCHOOL
WITS WRITER: BRIAN KETTLER

BETSY
*(bursts through saloon doors)* What in tarnation is going on here?

*(Pickett and Clementine stop making out and look at Betsy)*

BETSY
I thought you loved me, Pickett, I really did.

PICKETT
Betsy, darling, you know I do! Remember when I killed my first-ever longhorn cow bull? It was all for you, baby.

BETSY
Then what are you doing with HER?! *(points to Clementine and starts showing signs of rage)*

CLEMENTINE
We were kissing. *(sheepishly and innocently giggles)*

BETSY
*(mocks Clementine's laugh and quickly makes straight face)* You're telling me that you were seriously slurpin' the mouth of this yahoo?!

PICKETT
Well it wasn't quite slurpin' hun, it was more of a...uh...a peck! Like a mama bird helping out a lost bird!

BETSY
*(is not amused and crosses her arms)* And who were you in this situation?

PICKETT
The mama bird...you see, I came in here looking for some moonshine, but then I saw Clem-ey in here looking all beer and skittles. I was just trying to make her feel better.

CLEMENTINE

*(to Betsy)* Aw, you guys would be great for each other; it looks like you could use a lil' lovin.

BETSY

*(begins circling Pickett)* Okay, "mama bird." *(looks at Clementine)* "Lil bird."

*(Abraham Lincoln enters riding Dave, the friendly dinosaur)*

ABRAHAM LINCOLN

Four score and seven years ago...oh, what do we have here? Who are you?

BETSY

Abraham Lincoln! Well, anyways, Pickett here is cheating on me! *(points to Pickett)*

ABRAHAM LINCOLN

Who?

BETSY

*(points to Pickett)* Him! I just pointed. How is this pointing thing not clear to you?

PICKETT

Me?

ABRAHAM LINCOLN

You?

CLEMENTINE

No! Yes!

ABRAHAM LINCOLN

Order in the court, order in the court!

BETSY

We aren't in a courtroom.

ABRAHAM LINCOLN

I practiced law for years without a law degree; leave me to do my work here. See now, I believe I have come to understand the problem at hand. You two *(a dramatic flourish of awkward twisting and pointing)* Betsy,

Pickett, are having an issue. Please step forward and state your claim.

*(Dave roars)*

ABRAHAM LINCOLN
Oh settle down, Dave, being a few minutes late to your jazzercise class won't kill you.

BETSY
Well! I walked into the saloon here. I saw them two smoochin' and shouted, "What in tarnation is going on here?" and boy was I mad to see this!

PICKETT
Stop! Let me explain. I wasn't kissing HER! We were just touching LIPS!

ABRAHAM LINCOLN
Well, it seems to me we have a classic "cowboy cheats on cowgirl girlfriend by kissing the town yahoo" situation.

*(Dave roars)*

ABRAHAM LINCOLN
Dave, be patient! As the first president of the United States of America to have a beard, it is my civil duty to help these people.

BETSY
I want him exiled!

PICKETT
Exiled?!

ABRAHAM LINCOLN
Exiled

ABRAHAM LINCOLN
Egg salad?!

DAVE
*(sings in opera)* Exxxiiiilllleeeddd...

*(everyone looks at Dave in utter disbelief)*

ABRAHAM LINCOLN

Why, Dave, that was incredible! I didn't even know you could talk. Where did you learn to sing like that?!

DAVE

When you go out for oyster Thursday with the boys, I go to the community center. They give free opera singing lessons. I've been going for the past three years. I've been sneaking fliers for our monthly recitals on your desk, but you never come.

ABRAHAM LINCOLN

Oh, Dave, my trusty companion, I'm so sorry! I saw those fliers, but never knew they were from you, since, well, you are a dinosaur and I didn't think you had these cognitive abilities.

DAVE

It's okay, I understand.

ABRAHAM LINCOLN

No, it's not okay. Come my opera-singing, highly cognitively evolved friend, we have a lifetime of friendship to catch up on.

*(Dave and Abraham Lincoln walk off stage. Clementine, Pickett, and Betsy all exchange confused looks.)*

# I Feared

Maddie Hagan
GRANT HIGH SCHOOL
WITS WRITER: MARK POMEROY

When I was a kid I feared deep water swallowing me up,
the big kids at school, scraggly rats that lived in the alley behind my house,
earthquakes, thunderstorms that gave way to tornadoes, Hurricane Katrina,
my dog dying, my best friend forgetting me when I moved away,
airplanes taking off, spiders, bird-eating spiders from the zoo in Amsterdam,
the northern pike
that lived in my grandpa's lake,
the crawdads that lived in my grandpa's lake,
getting kidnapped, stepping behind the horses on the farm,
our existence not being real, eating food I don't like, growing up.
I feared my mom dying, not being able to make friends, elevators made of transparent glass,
speaking in front of people at school, getting my shoelace stuck in the escalator at the mall,
the metallic pinch of getting shots, getting teeth pulled, people talking about me behind my back,
getting amnesia like my grandma, alcohol, the earwigs in my rose bushes,
ghosts living in my house,
becoming a ghost.

## Interpretation

Sven Schilling
WILSON HIGH SCHOOL
WITS WRITER: BETTINA DE LEÓN BARRERA

A rough, frothy, blue snake of water that
Winds between mottled shades of green.
A random surge of direction.
Which way does it travel?
From the upper left to the lower right?
Or vice versa?
Could be done with oil pastel.
Rough, uncontained.
A changing sense of dimension.
A youthful green on the border of blue.
The ombre starting from the middle.
The Mood.
Crescendo or decrescendo?
Fortissimo or Pianissimo?
Mezzo-Piano.
A good calm.
What kinds of greens?
Coniferous trees.
A Calico green on a cat's back.
A blue spine skirting between the ribcage.
An eel.
My imagination?
A snail trail through the moss on the back
Of the road.
The side that hides from the sun.
A crisp, cool winter evening.
When the Sun's really out for once.
Just before Spring can take the wheel
Of the Season.
Layers.
Carved wax on a canvas.
Interpretation.

# My Neighborhood

Nathan Miller
ALLIANCE HIGH SCHOOL AT MEEK
WITS WRITER: LAURA MOULTON

This neighborhood never made me my best. If anything, it almost turned me into someone I'd never wanted to become.

Families of five or six lived in the small three-bedroom townhouses. The children often caused trouble when they were allowed outside. This meant stealing the neighbor's stuff, bikes, chairs, toys, etc. They would also fight to show off. There may have been some heavy drug use. We would ding-dong-ditch, light beer boxes on fire, throw pinecones at the other kids across the street. Sometimes late at night, we would hide in the bushes in the sniper position, with our airsoft guns, and we would shoot the cars passing by.

When high school came around, my house was the place to hang out. It was only for my close friends, but it was kind of like a "trap house." We spent our time getting high on marijuana and playing video games. I had to be saved.

Soon after freshman year, I left and never looked back. I am a better man now. I have goals now, I have a great life now. I was repaired, but I still have nostalgia about those times.

## My Wonderland Complex

*Recipient of the Tavern Books Prize for Poetry*

Ire McMichael
GRESHAM HIGH SCHOOL
WITS WRITER: JAMES GENDRON

Arsenic and sugar. Drink one, and you drink both, but
differently.

Differential: sugar is sweet, arsenic bitter.

Drink the arsenic, descend into your mind, dank, dark,
toxic, poisonous mind of a depressed teenager.

Drink the sugar, ascend into your heart, light, glowy, sweet
childlike mind of an emotional wreck.

Drink neither, and you become beige, bland, live out your
normal boring life, as if your tears and emotions are
dirt, nothing special.

Drink both, stay there but be here, act like only you, act
adventurously, bravely, confidently.

My suggestions? Drink both, from the infinite glass of the
Gods.

Be as if your tears are fire and diamonds.

Be passionate and rare.

# Jude & Finnley

*Recipient of the Glimmer Train Prize for Fiction*

Lily Boyd
GRANT HIGH SCHOOL
WITS WRITER: MARK POMEROY

The feeling of dread drips down my spine like a drop of cold water. I stand in front of the mirror, the early morning light filtering purple into my room. *You can do this*, I whisper. *You can, you can*, though with every word my voice becomes shakier. *Fuck.* I pinch out strands of my hair. *Fuck, calm down, calm down.*

"Finn," Mom calls up the stairs. "Honey, come on, you're gonna be late for the first day of school!"

"Coming," I reply, fear ringing plain in my voice.

"It's going to be great," Mom says. The car sputters to a half-hearted rumble. "You'll go to dances, you'll go to football games, soccer games, basketball!" The car stops at a red light and I feel her watching me. "You might even date a girl. There was one, I remember, what was her name, Mona? Monica? I know it started with an M, but she always liked you, didn't she? Maybe you could ask her to homecoming?" I nod as we pull up in front of school. "I love you honey," Mom says. Her eyes gleam, in sadness or pride, I can't tell. I smile at her before slinging my backpack over my shoulder. I smile all the way through the doors, up the stairs, into my first class. I smile and I hope and I wish for everything Mom wants me to be. And then the bell rings, and the world comes crashing down, and all the noise and all the worry comes flooding in.

I watch as each student shares what they did over the summer, hearing everything I didn't do, and when it's my turn, I simply shake my head, and no one is surprised. And that makes everything so much worse because I can feel the words, stuck in my throat. I can feel them right beneath the surface.

When his name is called I take a quick intake of breath. He snaps and unsnaps the bottom button of his shirt as he talks. His hair is blonder since last June when he said, "Bye, have a good summer" on the last day of school. I had choked out a surprised "You, too." It had been one of the best days of my life.

He was in my ceramics class last year when we got paired up for a project. He smelled of Lysol and olive oil. I wasn't sure I liked it, but I also didn't dislike it. He had smiled. "You're Finnley, right?" he'd said. "I'm Jude." I was so shocked he knew my name I could barely speak.

"Umm, yep, that's me."

We worked together every Wednesday for two months, building a model house out of everyday items. The day before we turned it in he touched my cheek,

"Thanks," he said.

"For what?" I asked, in a barely there voice.

He shrugged. "For being nice, I guess, for being not what I expected. Just, thanks." And I had thought for a moment that he would kiss me, but then the moment passed like moments do, and I didn't know what to say, so I said nothing, and he pulled his hand away. I felt my breath hitch and he smiled knowingly. But then the project was over and he would no longer catch my eye or rush to meet me on the way to the library after school. He was no longer mine and I was no longer his.

"Finnley, that's your name right?" The teacher, whose name I hadn't bothered to remember, smiles. "Are you sure you don't want to share? I'm sure you did something really exciting."

*Remember this is the year it changes, just stand up.* And I'm looking across a sea of expectant heads. *Say something.* And suddenly I'm talking, and I don't even know what I'm saying because all I did this summer was work at the forest service and dodge my mom's questions about when my buddies were going to come over. But I'm talking, and she's nodding and smiling, so it must be good. And then I'm done, and as I'm sitting down I glance over at him, but he's getting something from his backpack and doesn't see me. I can tell exactly where he is, two rows over. *Just take a peek, what if he's looking at you and you're missing it? But then what if he is looking at you, and then you look, and it's awkward and you ruin everything?* So I don't look. Then the teacher is talking again, and the bell rings, splitting the silence like the rip of paper, and everyone's moving, and all I can focus on is the frenzied crush of people and the buzz of the fluorescents and the smell of perfume and sweat.

I slip into the bathroom closest to me, falling into a stall, locking the door behind me with shaky fingers. For a moment I feel safe.

After school, Mom glances at me worriedly, nervous energy turning the air static. "It was good?" she finally bursts, as we idle at a yellow light. "Your first day, was it good?"

I shrug. "I shared what I did over the summer in English, and sat with this new kid at lunch." That last part wasn't true. I ate outside like I always did. Nobody ever went out there because it was only highway and an abandoned strip mall, but that's why I liked it, it was only me.

"Finn, that's amazing," she says. "Tell me everything. I told you this year would be different, didn't I tell you that? I just knew it!" I nod. "We need to celebrate. I'm supposed to take the evening shift, but I'll call Becky, I'm sure she'll take it. Lord knows I've covered for her..."

§

The kitchen is small—a yellow table shoved against the wall, the faint smell of mildew permeating the air. "My card wouldn't clear at the store," Mom says, grabbing two plates from the cupboard. "But we'll make do." She pulls out packages from a Wendy's bag, leaving crescents of grease shining on the counter. "I got a variety of stuff because, you know, we're celebrating." And then she smiles, so I smile back, though all I feel is the dull twist of familiarity. We sit at the yellow table eating in silence, the faint rumble of passing cars filtering through the quiet.

"This is really good," I say.

"Thanks, Finn," she says, smiling sadly.

Nighttime is always the worst. I lie in bed, unable to sleep, unable to shut my brain off, my mind latching on to every gurgle of the pipes or sirens in the night. I get up before dawn, clumsily reaching for the bottle of pills at the back of my dresser.

"For emergencies," the doctor had said as he pressed the bottle into my mother's hand. She had frowned, and my heart had sunk. Finally my fingers find the bottle, and I shake one of the rust-colored pills into my palm, swallowing it dry. Emergencies were becoming more common lately.

I'm walking to chemistry when he grabs my arm. I'm so surprised I let out a yell and immediately feel a blush pulse into my cheeks when I see him. He laughs, his freckles raising into a smile.

"Um, hi," I say.

"Hey," he says.

My heart is beating so fast I can feel it thrum through my entire body.

"This Friday, there's this thing, I think it would be, um, cool if you came. Do you wanna do that?"

I can't speak. He glances around nervously. "Do you wanna do that?" he says again.

*Talk, say something goddamn it, you wanna go, just talk.* "Yes, sure, that would be amazing." I grin.

"Great," he says. And then the bell rings. And I've completely forgot we're at school, or that I'm a nobody, or that I'm supposed to be sad. "I'll text you," he says, still smiling. "I'll text you everything you need to know, so, yeah, Friday."

"Friday," I repeat. I watch him walk away until he turns the corner. He doesn't look back.

§

*2036 NE Maplewood.* The message flashes across my screen thirty minutes later. My phone buzzes again. *Do you need a ride?* My fingers shake so hard I can barely type a response. *Yes,* I write, but is that too strong? I delete it. *Sure, thanks.* I pace around my room, waiting for the doorbell, wringing my clammy hands. Mom is working the night shift at the hospital. I hadn't told her what was going on; my first party. The three chimes ring through the house and I glance in the mirror one last time, the crescent moon birthmark on my cheek winking nervously back, before running down the stairs.

"Hey," he says, looking up from the doorstep.

"Hey," The oatmeal-colored van horn honks, and I look past him.

"Hurry up, assholes!" someone yells from inside and someone else, a girl I think, laughs. He rolls his eyes. "You coming?" he says over his shoulder. "They'd leave us behind in a fucking heartbeat."

I laugh, feeling the sound like something exotic roll down my throat.

It's a warm night, with lingering summer air breezing through the dark. When we pull in front of the house everyone scrambles to the doors, practically falling over each other to get out. He gets out before me.

I see him talking animatedly to one of his friends, a tall girl with curly brown hair. I expected I'd be able to see lights, smell smoke, hear music. I expected I'd be able to taste the party just looking at the house; I can't. It's an ugly mud color, with an overgrown garden spilling onto the pavement. I make my way up the cement walk on the outskirts of the group. Bits of conversation drift back to me. I've seen all these people before, but I don't know a single name and I can tell by the way they glance at me that they're wondering why I'm here. I don't blame them; I'm beginning to wonder myself.

It's dark inside, the blinds drawn tight over the windows. Pale purple light from a single bulb bathes everything in a surreal haze. A dozen kids are strewn out on a tan couch, others standing against the walls. Voices sift whispery through the halls. Smoke tangles around my lungs, making the air thick, mixing with the sickly sweet smell of vomit.

"Hey, you made it. What the fuck took you so long?" A gangly boy wraps an arm around Jude's shoulder. He's taller than Jude with thin, freckly arms and wild unkempt hair. I don't think I like him. "Did you bring the shit?" he asks, his voice conspiring, and everyone laughs.

Jude grins, pulling a crumpled Ziploc bag from his back pocket, a few blunts lying limp at the bottom. The boy smiles, grabbing the baggie from Jude's hand. I feel my back hit the wall, realizing I've been walking backwards. My head hurts. I wander through the rooms watching as smoke curls from darkened lips and flat beer sinks past their tongues. A low bass thrums, the hardwood floor rumbling beneath my feet, and then I see him. His head is bent away, and he's wiping his nose on the back of his hand.

It's too hot, it's too loud, the crush of people makes my skin itch. I push open the back door, the air cool against my sweat-slicked forehead. I feel as if a hand has slipped down my throat and is slowly compressing my ribs, pinching my heart. I sink against the chain-link fence, staring up at the sky, closing my eyes, listening to the rush of blood in my ears. It feels like a long time before I open them again. I hear his voice before I see him.

"Finnley?" he says, his voice slurred, wavering. When he sees me he smiles, plopping down by my side. "Hey," he says. His eyes are red and slightly unfocused, he smells soft, like incense. "Hey," he says again.

But I can't say anything because I can't stop looking at him, and I can't open my mouth because that would break this moment of peace, and I don't want to risk it.

"You know," he says, not bothered by my silence. "You know, I always notice you looking at me in class, like out of the corner of your eye." When he feels my body stiffen, he laughs. "No, you don't understand," he whispers. "I like it, I'm fine with it." My heart beats into my head, and I can feel his body next to mine. "I like it," he says again.

And suddenly I don't care that I'm cold, or tired, or that I shouldn't be here because his head is next to mine. I can feel his breath warm on my cheek, and then I feel his lips on mine, and I can taste the smoke on his saliva mixing with something sharp. I want to stay here forever, and for a moment I believe we will, but then he pulls away, and I'm left staring at his beautiful face. He smiles. "I like it." His eyes drift to the ground. We sit there for a long time. At some point he falls asleep, his head lolling on my shoulder. I barely breathe not wanting to wake him up, and I never want the night to end.

I don't hear from him over the weekend. They told me they would take care of him, that he always slept at their house after a party, that it was fine. I caught the bus home, the last of the night. It was so warm, so quiet, so beautiful, and I felt as if I would burst, watching the sky blur into the trees out of the smudged window.

I wake up the next morning in a cold panic convinced I dreamed it all up. Saturday, he doesn't text. When Sunday passes and my phone lays silent, I start to worry. What if something happened to him? He was so out of it, why didn't I help him home? I just left him there. Then again, why should I be worried?

*He's not texting because he doesn't like you, he never liked you.*

I take two pills before bed.

Monday morning, we hit every red light going to school. I savor every second I get to spend in the car, my body tight with panic. *He hasn't texted, he doesn't like you, never did, never will.*

Then I remember his lips, the way his fingers brushed mine, his head on my shoulder, and I have to bite my tongue to keep from smiling.

He walks in ten minutes late to first period and for some reason I feel as if everyone is staring at me. Do they know? Later, I catch him looking at me and for a second our eyes meet, but he looks away.

After class, he pushes his chair back too hard, banging into the desk behind him, grabbing his backpack and walking out of the room before I even stand up. I see his head bobbing down the hallway. I race to catch up with him, darting outside into the chill morning. He's walking towards the overpass when I reach him. He doesn't seem surprised that I'm there, but he doesn't seem happy either.

"Hey," he says. "What are you doing out here? I didn't think you were the type to skip." I don't know what to say, I don't know where to start. But the reserved look on his face punctures my confidence.

"I just wanted to know," I breathe, my words sounding jittery. "I wanted to know what this is. I know at the party we were something, but now we're not, and I don't know what that means."

He stops walking and doesn't look at me. "Look," he finally says. "Look, I don't know what you think happened, or what you think I did that night, but I was pretty fucked up. Even if something did happen, it didn't really happen, not really." He looks up, the expression on his face is so sad I don't know what to say. "It didn't happen," he says again, though now more to himself. Neither one of us says anything for a long time. I feel as if my insides are slowly turning to sludge.

"I gotta catch the bus," he says, finally walking away.

I stand there for what seems like hours, listening to the cars on the highway, and the sound of my heart pounding.

He isn't in class the next day, and then not again, not again, not again.

I text him *I'm sorry*, yet I have no idea what I am apologizing for. He doesn't text back.

A week after he kissed me in the dark, I start to feel desperate. I call him late Saturday night, my heart banging in my chest. He doesn't pick up; my blood goes static.

After that I stop trying. *You should have seen this coming. Why would you get your hopes up? Why would someone like Jude like you?*

He's in class on Monday, but it doesn't matter anymore. Every time I glance at him, his eyes are fixed forward.

I stop sleeping—my days one long blur of exhaustion. Two weeks later, I refill my bottle of pills.

"Finn." Mom pulls out of the pharmacy parking lot. It rained earlier, and everything smells like dirt. "Let's go out to eat. I've been working so much. We need something good."

"Sure," I say. "Let's get Chinese."

We park the car on the street and walk in. The restaurant smells like old oil and orange and everything is red. Paper lanterns hang from the ceilings and pictures of dragons with glittering gold scales are stuck to the walls. The carpet is a deep maroon. We sit in silence as we wait for our food.

And then I hear his voice, and I look over, and he's right there, tucked into the corner booth. He's laughing, and all I want to know is who's making him laugh like that? Why can't I?

We're getting our food when they stand up to leave and my heart tumbles from my chest.

It's one of the girls from the party, with the brown hair and mocha complexion. He hands her her coat before wrapping an arm around her shoulders. As they're walking toward the door I swear he sees me, but then again, maybe not. She has her head nuzzled against his collarbone, and he's laughing again.

I can hear it even when the door closes behind them.

## What I Will

Nancy Serrano
FRANKLIN HIGH SCHOOL
WITS WRITER: DAVID CIMINELLO

I will not stand your judgments
over what one person of my race did

I will speak up
when you call me a *pandillero*
or a drug dealer a.k.a. *narco*

I will not let you insult me
or *mi gente* for being "illegal" immigrants

I will not let you assume
my race because of my pale white skin tone

I will stop you when I hear
any sort of racist joke against any race

I will speak up
and you best believe I will
not stand any more discrimination
because of what one person did
or our skin colors

One person's actions do not mean
we will all do the same
a person's skin tone or birthplace
does not mean we are a certain race
a legal or illegal immigrant

## Dear Halima

Kerim Semed
LINCOLN HIGH SCHOOL
WITS WRITER: AMY MINATO

*(Context: Halima is my first cousin. She is now six months old. This is a poem to give her my take on a specific aspect of life that she will experience as she gets older.)*

Dear Halima,

Welcome to Earth
To the world in which we breathe and walk in
The world in which millions of mysteries wait before you

Millions of beautiful and pleasant experiences
But at the cost of hardships and turmoil
See this world isn't perfect, nor will it ever be
All of our flaws define us just as much as our strengths

Both often shaped and transformed based on external forces
That go by several names
Each unique and different in their own way

There's one named Joy
Joy will make it its life goal to please you
For you to see the world in a bright yellow light
Illuminate you to the dazzling colors that inhabit this world

But Joy isn't perfect
Joy, if necessary, will spread lies
Feed you with junk phrases
Use that same light to blind you for what the world truly is

But after meeting Joy, you'll eventually meet her brother
Grief

He can appear scary at one glance
But can give you the reality you deserve

Grief wipes the dust out of your eyes
Matures you and creates a
Rigid soul
That strengthens and solidifies you

But Grief isn't perfect
Grief often will ram into you
And if you aren't holding onto the rails to keep you balanced
It consumes you

As you get older, Halima
Be prepared to answer the door
As both Joy and Grief will occasionally come to see you

Don't dismiss or ignore them
As they will only knock harder
Let them in, talk with them
Get to know and understand why they are there

And eventually they will escort themselves to the exit
And leave you to continue your lifelong journey

I hope for the best
And wish you luck

# Italian Living

Ani Moss
GRESHAM HIGH SCHOOL
WITS WRITER: COURTENAY HAMEISTER

Living in an Italian household is definitely one of the most difficult, interesting, and amazing experiences I have ever had. It consists of having a half-hour long debate about whether to have angel hair or spaghetti pasta with your *squarcharella* (a delicious Italian pasta dish with ham and eggs that definitely goes best with linguini, however I don't say anything because that will only delay dinner several more hours).

This brings me to the point that when living with Italians you can say *sayonara* to ever being on time. When we have to be somewhere at 3:00 my mom will start getting ready at 2:59.

Another thing you can expect are exaggerated hand gestures that seem nonsensical and frankly a little goofy, but if you look close enough can help tell the story of what their words are telling you. Living in an Italian household teaches you that when your mom is upset, her idea of "talking about it" is skipping the talking and yelling at the top of her lungs, again with the exaggerated hand gestures. This may be an everyday occurrence if you are close with someone that contains the hot-blooded Mediterranean genes.

Italian living is always expecting guests and knowing that if someone is coming over, you'll have to clean the entire house spotless as well as put together an elaborate tray of cheese, salami, prosciutto and other antipasto, even if the person is only coming for a couple minutes. If any of these tasks are not completed within an hour of the guests' arrival time you can refer back to my previous statement about Italian mother's yelling.

And if you ever have to go out somewhere with the family for birthdays, holidays, or soccer games (these tend to be the largest form of an Italian gathering), you can expect to spend at least four or more hours past the time your mom told you that you'd be home. Screaming, loud laughter, and annoyed glares from surrounding people are a party essential when it comes to Italian get-togethers. A gathering of Italians is rowdy, hectic and all the other synonyms for just plain crazy and wild behavior you can think of. Crazy is definitely a common theme when it comes to living in an Italian household.

In an Italian family you never know what to expect, like how I never expected to learn so much from being a part of this community. Living with Italians has taught me to look at the little things, like the differences between pastas or the five salamis in my fridge that all look exactly the same but have incredibly unique flavors. I've learned how to be respectful, hardworking, and how to have a good time at every event.

Home life, or just life in general is never dull when you you're with Italians. It may not always be fun and the best time you've ever had, but you definitely will never be bored. Out of everything I've learned in my eighteen years, the most important lesson is that it's okay to be just a little bit bonkers, because that makes life a heck of a lot more fun.

# What

Axel Dole
BENSON HIGH SCHOOL
WITS WRITER: KATHLEEN LANE

Me and Toam had just gotten married. It wasn't a conventional marriage though, not in a church, and not Vegas style.

"We'll run off together, then find a minister and a field."

"What about other attendees?"

"Do you really want your mother to come see us get married? She already doesn't like me as a fiancé."

"Oh, all right."

We went to our normal day jobs. He worked at a law firm; I was a studio technician. We both agreed to not eat anything that day or the day before. We wanted our first meal as newlyweds to be the most enjoyable. He was going to come home that night and pack. I, on the other hand, was going to leave work and get the car ready. I packed the day before.

"Hey, babe."

"What?"

"Don't forget your birthday suit; we need to look good for the photos."

"What's wrong with you."

We were going to fly. Not a national flight, but international. To France. It had been thought over by both of us, for a while. We both knew Latin; it wouldn't be that hard to figure out the language. He would talk English to me, but our style of Latin-French to the natives. Same for me to him.

"Are you ready?"

"Whenever you are."

"It should be just a few more minutes."

"Alright."

Get rid of the car. That was what we would do. Drive to the airport, and wire the pedal so it would go into the river. They would think us dead. Burn the house as well. It wasn't really a looker. We were ready.

"Alright, let's go."

"Are you sure about this?"
"What do you mean, of course I am."
"Good."

Staring at the house in the mirror was a beautiful image. The yellow-orange flames licking the trees. The neighbors would be alright. They had some fancy fire alarms that would immediately call the fire department if they went off. It would be alright. We were alright.

"Those flames do look big though."
"Do you think we should turn around?"
"No, we don't want to miss the flight. They'll be alright."
"They'll be alright."

They weren't. The flames had gotten the power lines. They melted and the alarms never went off. We were stopped at the gate. The police took us in and questioned us. What had happened. Wondered where we were going.

"I feel terrible."
"I know, me too."
"Should we confess?"
"No, they'll let us go now."

They took our story. We had just left to go to France and left the stove on. We still had the car. Toam refused to run it into the river. He was an environmentalist. A fire would likely suffice. No one could convict us.

"That's it?"
"I guess so."
"So we leave now."
"Yeah?"

We were happy. Our parents were not.

We occasionally read their updates. They mourned us. We managed to fake our deaths. Burnt the car. Mostly, we successfully eloped.

## Boredom

Griffin Blanton
ROOSEVELT HIGH SCHOOL
WITS WRITER: JOANNA ROSE

Boredom is a middle-aged man
with brown hair and stone-colored clothes
sitting in the middle of an empty room
staring at the ceiling
searching for something to look at
in the sea of nothingness.
Alas, he never finds anything
but he'll keep looking because
what else is there to do?

# Mexico

Frank Romanaggi
CLEVELAND HIGH SCHOOL
WITS WRITER: ALEX BEHR

The cobblestone streets of San Miguel De Allende shone in the March sunlight as they had been worn down over hundreds of years.

"Where's our house, GG?" I asked.

"It's right up there, the one with the biggest door."

As I ran ahead all I saw were tiny colorful doors; I imagined elves coming out of them.

"This house is tiny!" I yelled as I saw our front door.

"It looks that way from the front because the surrounding houses are visually compressing it, but from the back it spreads inside the whole block."

She was right. The house was incredible. Vibrant colors surrounded the house like a *piñata*. Arched glass doors framed the enclosed courtyard. Ginormous rich brown stairs hugged the wall leading up to a balcony as big as the house next door. The view was unbelievable. Sky-high churches replaced skyscrapers as they towered over children in blue colorful uniforms playing in the garden.

"GG, this church is huge," I yelled down the stairs. The historic pink church, surrounded by green trees, rose from the center of the rainbow houses.

"It's the Parroquia de San Miguel."

In the afternoons we would take a trip down to the Mercado Juan de Dios. As we were walking down the street, we carried woven plastic multi-colored bags to hold our upcoming purchases.

In the *mercado* we would be greeted by Herrardo who would offer us samples of his fresh fruits and vegetables. My favorite was the *granada de china*, a fruit that I had never tasted nor seen before in my life. The hard orange outer shell protects the inner slimy flesh that coats the addictive seeds that crunch in your mouth.

As we walked deeper into the *mercado*, past the fruit and vegetables, we entered into the flower section that had every color and scent imaginable. After a sharp right turn we entered the main arena. Before us lay an abundance of goods: fresh herbs for curing any ailment, toys, cowboy hats, hand-painted pottery, candy, tools, leather goods, boots and shoes, fresh honey, hand-woven carpets, glassware, trinkets, lams and furniture, *¡y mucho mucho mas!*

In Mexico the main meal is often served in the early afternoon around two o' clock. This meal is called *comida*. Dinner, or *cena* is often very light.

Teresa the cook would ask, "*¿Qué quieres para cenar?*"

Our brief debate would involve savory Mexican dishes and often we would resolve the debate by asking Teresa for *una sorpresa*...a surprise.

Come dinnertime we would gather around the ten-foot table in the shadow of my grandmother's "unfinished women" painting. After dinner, my Poppy would build a fire in the *sala abierta* that overlooks the dark blue tiled swimming pool accompanied by the relaxing sound of the fountain. Above us the stars appeared much brighter due to the 6,500-foot altitude and the absence of big city lights.

After we had time to digest our dinner, we would take a walk to *el centro* where we would buy an ice cream from one of many street vendors and watch performers as they entertained the people. As you surveyed the scene, you would see many *mariachi* bands in contrast to the break-dancers, fire dancers, balloon vendors, and singers of varying talents. Open-air restaurants surround the central *jardin*. In the middle of all the action lay a magnificent bandstand where on occasion people would perform. The general atmosphere of central San Miguel is nothing short of magical.

After all the excitement we would venture home to put on our PJs. Late in the night when everyone was asleep my sister and I would sneak up to the rooftop terrace. The feel of the concrete roof was cold yet comforting. The sound of monstrous fireworks boomed through the silence of the town. Red, yellow, blue, and purple pierced the sky. The view of houses almost stacked on top of each other was like no other. It was Mexico and it was beautiful.

## Trashcan

Elena Iven
ALLIANCE HIGH SCHOOL AT MEEK
WITS WRITER: LAURA MOULTON

He yells at me to cook for him as he sits
on his chair acting like a spoiled child.

The times I see my family at gatherings with
bear face and raggedy clothes look at me, whispering,
*she should be more ladylike.*

But the weight in my heart keeps telling me to get out!
to discover who I am, not what they want me to become.

I am brave, I am strong, I'm not the girl
waiting in the trash can.

Always carrying a Taser with me when I go outside, it's
not for show, not to look cool, but for my protection,
because we are considered weak, powerless creatures.
Even though what separates us from them are the name tags.

I'm not the girls waiting in the trashcan.

Generations through generations we are subconsciously
teaching our kids what they should be, not what they are already.
But is our generation to blame? Are we the ones carrying on these traditions?

Am I just a pawn waiting in the trashcan for instructions?

Every day is the same, scared to get up, to go outside to see society's
burning gases.
For the ones who are about to conceive, do they know what they are
bringing them into?

Who is the one waiting in the trashcan?

We have had enough! We are the ones keeping our population up, not you!
Without us you are nothing. You should bring me a chair to sit in.
You should be trusted so we don't have to carry lighting sticks around.

If you think about it like that
are we the ones throwing them in the trashcan?
What the words are feeding you on those electrifying boxes aren't true.
All we want is to be treated the same as you. Is that so hard to understand?
We want peace not chaos, we have to work together to keep this planet going.
It's not just you, it's not just us, it's both.

I get it, it's us climbing out of what seemed like a closed trashcan lid
But it's now open, and it will always stay open.

We are the ones standing outside of the trashcan.

## When it Rains it Reminds Me of You

Melieah Tanner
ROOSEVELT HIGH SCHOOL
WITS WRITER: JOANNA ROSE

The pencil moves on paper
on paper like people
who heal themselves
Dark shadows and fights.

## Mask

Xinyu Shi
LINCOLN HIGH SCHOOL
WITS WRITER: LISA EISENBERG

WHY!!
STOP CRYING... YOU HAVE TO ACCEPT THE REALITY MY DEAR
YOU CAN NOT CHANGE THE SOCIETY, BUT YOU CAN CHANGE YOURSELF TO FIT IN THE SOCIETY.
OR, YOU WILL BE ISOLATED FOREVER
YOU HAVE TO CUT YOUR LONG HAIR, DYE YOUR HAIR IN THE STANDARD PATTERN, AND WEAR SCHOOL UNIFORM
...
GOOD MORNING, NICE TO MEET YOU! MY NAME IS GABY!

ME TOO....
I FEEL A LITTLE BIT TIRED, I NEED TO GO HOME NOW. SEE YOU LATER.
WE DON'T KNOW WHEN WE CAN STOP WEARING THE MASKS BEFORE WE USED TO. I.T.

## E Pluribus Unum

Dyllan Newville
ROOSEVELT HIGH SCHOOL
WITS WRITER: JOANNA ROSE

Hands of all the shades of the earth
all the way from deep browns
located adjacent
to the broiling core of our earth
to the puffy white clouds disappearing
as the lines of geese make their way south
although the range of colors is as vast as the sea
every complexion is laced with the undertone of hope
as we all join together
making up the foundation of something new
on a land with as much variety
as the people who roam
yet only to be broken down again
by those worshipping the clouds

## The Appearance

Ysabella Chilton, Nhan Doan, Kim Le, & Vy Tran
BENSON HIGH SCHOOL
WITS WRITER: MONTY MICKELSON

CHARACTERS

SONY: Asian American teenage boy, best friends with Bella, very sassy and oblivious.

BELLA: white teenage girl, best friends with Sony.

EXTERIOR CHURCH - DAY

*(On a typical Sunday, two friends walk into a church to attend mass and pray.)*

INTERIOR CHURCH - CHAPEL - DAY

*(The two friends enter a chapel and kneel in one of the empty rows. After praying, the two friends head out of the chapel. As the two friends walk about of the chapel, Sony stops and finds a bracelet on the floor and picks it up. Bella walks out of the chapel. Sony puts on the bracelet and leaves the chapel to find where Bella went.)*

EXTERIOR CHURCH - HALLWAY - DAY

*(Sony walks down the hallway and attempts to call Bella to find out where she went. The church facility is empty with little to no sight of other people. Sony heads to the bathroom to take a quick bathroom break before continuing to look for Bella.)*

INTERIOR CHURCH - BATHROOM - DAY

*(After finishing his business, Sony takes off the bracelet and washes his hands. Sony turns off the faucet and tries to grab a paper towel, but the paper towel dispenser is jammed. As Sony is attempting to unjam the paper towel dispenser, the faucet turns on by itself.)*

GHOST

*(giggles)*

SONY

*(turns off the faucet and continues to unjam the paper towel dispenser)* Oh, there you go. *(fixes the paper towel dispenser and puts the bracelet back on)*

GHOST

*(giggles)*

SONY

I'm scared now, I need to leave. *(leaves the bathroom)*

EXTERIOR CHURCH - HALLWAY - DAY

SONY

*(walks down the hallway and attempts to call Bella again)* Where is everybody? Oh my gosh! *(walks out of the hallway)*

EXTERIOR CHURCH FACILITY - DAY

SONY

*(takes a seat after having trouble finding Bella)* Oh my gosh. *(takes out his phone and goes on social media)*

*(The ghost walks up and stands behind Sony. Sony goes on Snapchat and takes a selfie to post on his story. After checking social media for a while, Sony gets a snap back from a friend.)*

FRIEND

What is that to your right?

SONY

*(re-checks the selfie he took to see what his friend was talking about)* Oh my gosh, what the F is that? *(looks around himself to find there is nothing but plants surrounding him)* What is this? But I look cute though! *(continues to look around himself making sure nothing is there)* I'm scared now. I need to leave. *(stands up and looks for Bella again)*

EXTERIOR CHURCH - PARKING LOT - DAY

*(Bella and Sony reunite with each other in the parking lot of the church facility)*

SONY

But like I find something inside the chapel, but I think it's like really bad. Cause it looks old, but it's like kind of weird. It looks like this. *(takes off the bracelet and shows it to Bella)*

BELLA

Oh my gosh. You need to put that back. That's not okay. *(pushes the bracelet in Sony's hand away from herself)*

SONY
Really?

BELLA
Like I don't trust if you pick something random up, that's really creepy. Like, you picked up that from the church like that? That might be...it might be belong to someone. Like, I don't know about that. It's kind of creepy.

SONY
Finders keepers. That's their loss. Not my problem...Okay, maybe you're right. Cause it's like so ratchet, and it's not even that cute. Like, what the F are these? Like are these freaking fake diamonds? *(tosses the bracelet into the bushes)*

EXTERIOR - SONY'S CAR - DAY
*(Bella and Sony head to the Sony's car)*

SONY
So, you want a ride?

BELLA
Yeah.

*(They chitchat as they get into the car to leave the church facility. As they are driving out away from the church facility, the ghost stands next to a tree and watches the two friends leave the parking lot.)*

INTERIOR SONY'S HOUSE - DAY
*(Sony gets home after driving Bella home from church. Sony sets down his phone on a nearby drawer, which also has the bracelet on it. Sony takes off his shoes and jacket without noticing the bracelet.)*

INTERIOR SONY'S HOUSE - BATHROOM - DAY
*(Sony walks into the bathroom look at his phone. The ghost stands in the bathroom behind him. Sony rinses the gel out of his hair and fixes up himself. He leaves the bathroom without seeing the ghost.)*

GHOST
*(giggles)*

INTERIOR SONY'S HOUSE - LIVING ROOM - DAY
*(Sony sits on the couch and turns on the TV)*

SONY

What should I watch today? Gossip girl? Grey's Anatomy? Oh my gosh, let's do Gossip Girl. I haven't watched that thing in such a long time. That's so junior year right there. *(watches Gossip Girl)* Oh my gosh! Dang girl, chill. You need-a like co-lax. Take a chill pill, girl, like, that's not how you play sports. So, chill. Oh my gosh. I need to snapchat this. *(picks up his phone out of the cup holder and finds the bracelet under his phone)* What is this doing here? I thought I threw this out. *(picks up the bracelet and looks at it)* I'm so creeped out. *(gets out of the chair and leaves the living room)*

EXTERIOR SONY'S HOUSE - FRONT YARD - DAY

SONY

*(runs out of his house onto the front yard)* Oh hell no. *(calls Bella)*

EXTERIOR BELLA'S HOUSE – DAY – INTERCUT PHONE CONVERSATION

*(phone rings)*

BELLA

*(picks up phone)* Hello?

SONY

Oh my gosh. Come over. You cannot believe this. Like things been happening to me and it's so creepy. Oh my gosh. I'm so freaking scared. Come over here. I need your help right now. Oh my gosh.

BELLA

Okay. I'll come over as fast as I can.

SONY

Well come fast. Oh my gosh.

BELLA

Okay.

SONY

Okay. Bye.

BELLA

Bye. *(leaves her house)*

SONY'S HOUSE - FRONT YARD - DAY

SONY

*(walks up to Bella's car)* Where have you been? I've been waiting for you. Can't believe you. What is wrong with you?

BELLA

Sorry I wasn't trying to get a speeding ticket today.

SONY

Oh my gosh.

*(Bella leaves her car and Sony leads her into his house, telling her about the happenings. Sony leads Bella upstairs into the* LIVING ROOM, *telling her about the happenings.)*

SONY

So, yea, it's like scary in this room. It's like all of a sudden cold. And it's just like creepy. It's like, like haunted. Yeah, so, oh my god, yeah, right there. That's it. *(shows Bella where he found the bracelet)*

GHOST

*(giggles)*

*(Bella starts running away from the bracelet, dragging Sony along with her)*

SONY

Oh my gosh, I told you we should have gotten out of here.
*(Bella and Sony run towards the stairs. They stop at the top of the stairs to see the ghost standing there.)*

GHOST

*(giggles)* Boo.

FADE OUT

## Sting

Isabelle Jacqmotte-Parks
CLEVELAND HIGH SCHOOL
WITS WRITER: ALEX BEHR

"Ready, set, go!" My friend, Madeleine, shouted gleefully, running toward Clinton Street as she dramatically clutched her green plastic water gun. Her long, walnut hair fluttered to frame her face as she glanced back at us, an expression of excitement and determination crossing her face. Anticipation replaced her gap-toothed grin as she waited for us to scatter. A moment of silence passed before I darted, shrieking like a banshee, to the opposite side of the house, where the small stone path crawled by leafy, green hedges, and a tall oak fence stood, the boundary for all our adventures. Ava, the sweetest of the three, and Sophia, the most competitive (rivaled only by Madeleine), both disappeared into the backyard in a blur of blond hair, tennis shoes and brightly colored T-shirts. They maneuvered around various soccer balls and basketballs, past the row of radiant, fragrant, blooming lavender and honeysuckle, and the dilapidated basketball hoop.

Even with the welcome comfort of the shade, I felt the dry, Portland summer heat seep into my skin. My arms reeked of the SPF 50 Coppertone sunscreen my mother had slathered on that morning. Ava squealed in surprise from somewhere in the backyard; judging from the volume, I predicated she was near the garden boxes, which were filled with ripe, juicy tomatoes, the first crop of the summer.

I carefully examined the sunshine-summoned freckles that were speckling my gangly fifth-grade body. The purple Nerf Super Soaker I had hurriedly snatched lay beside me, cast aside in the lull of the shade. My reverie was rudely punctuated by Sophia's footsteps, thundering up the driveway as they pursued Madeleine.

Suddenly, a thud echoed across the yard, along with some mild yelling. Deciding to investigate, I stealthily crawled across the yard, my harmless weapon clutched tightly in my sweaty fingers. I crept behind a bush, unsuccessfully attempting to camouflage myself. I watched reverently as Madeleine shrieked, flailing her arms in an attempt to reach her dropped gun, Sophia mercilessly spraying her with lukewarm water. Madeleine's orange shirt was thoroughly drenched, and her beautiful hair had been reduced to a tangly, soggy clump. Sophia looked no better, her sopping, strawberry blond hair framing her expression of determination and subtle anger, dripping onto her striped shirt and blue sneakers. I was so focused on their bedraggled appearance, I failed to notice Ava creeping up behind me.

"Gotcha!" she hollered, pulling the trigger on her pink squirt gun. Startled, I slipped and wound up lying on the ground, trying to defend myself with my own gun as she relentlessly soaked me, from my strawberry blond curls to my plastic flip-flops. Eventually, our guns emptied, we stood there for a few seconds, unsure of how to proceed. After a few heartbeats of awkward silence, punctuated by giggles, Ava and I sprinted in opposite directions.

After reloading in the communal bucket, I followed a shrill, deafening scream to the driveway. I peeked around the corner of the house towards Madeleine and Sophia. Sophia had tripped by the garage, much like my own clumsy attempt at escape, and Madeleine was aiming her loaded Super Soaker at Sophia's relatively dry T-shirt. Suddenly I let out a cry, galloping at a furious pace towards the pair. They both swiveled to stare at me, a pair of blue eyes and a pair of brown eyes, the carefree energy evaporating as I yowled like a madman, mouth open as far as my jaw would allow. I was vaguely aware of a streak of purple in my peripheral vision and a subtle buzzing noise as I neared the end of the driveway.

Abruptly, something no bigger than a bean or a stone, grazed my lip. I stopped running, shocked, and began probing my mouth with my tongue. An agonizing pain shot through my cheek. Panic began to set in. Instinctively, I spat on the ground, doubling over with the effort. It hurt like nothing I'd felt before. I sprayed saliva across the cracked pavement of the driveway, panic and desperation clouding my thoughts. What was it? The pain escalated, almost numbing the inside of my cheek. It hurt so much. I couldn't think. Big, salty tears began to stream down my cheeks as I coughed and gagged. Why hadn't it fallen out? I cried out in pain. Madeleine, Ava, and Sophia all sprinted towards me, their weapons left lying on the ground, forgotten in their frenzy.

"What's going on? What's wrong?" they chorused, confusion and worry coloring their voices. Ava tentatively wrapped her arms around my shaking, folded body, trying to comfort me. From my stooped position, I caught a glimpse of Madeleine bolting towards the house, hair flying in her wake. I choked back a sob, feeling the pain spread across my cheek with every tremor. Finally, the object flew out of my mouth and onto the pavement. I received only minor relief, but the panic was gone.

"Isabelle?" A fourth voice echoed across the yard, alarm tinting their tone. I looked up, tears still clouding my vision. Mo, Ava's mother, rushed over to me, her dark brown eyes brimming with concern.

"What happened, honey? Can you tell me?" she pleaded, kneeling on the pavement in front of me. Madeleine and Sophia waited behind her, each whispering to the other; Madeleine nervously fiddled with the perfumed, overgrown rosemary bush as Sophia hurried to glance at my saliva-covered projectile.

"Oh, no!" she gasped as she examined it with the care of a surgeon. "Isabelle, that was a bee!" Madeleine and Sophia gasped in unison, while Mo simply nodded and sighed.

"Okay, honey, why don't we just go get a nice, cold cloth? I bet you'll feel much better after that, and I've heard baking soda might do the trick." Mo gently led my tear-blinded, pain-ridden self into their kitchen, where she gingerly spread baking soda across the inside of my cheek. I could feel the pain fading, but the taste was disgusting, so I pleaded that she let me use a cool cloth instead after a few minutes of the baking soda.

"All right. I'm just going to leave you here for a minute, okay? I'm going to call your parents and let them know what happened." She smiled at me, praised my tough nature, and left to find her phone.

While she was away, I slowly came to a realization. I'd thought that now I would hate bees more than before, but this proved to be an incorrect hypothesis on my part.

Instead, I found myself feeling sorry for the bee. It had only been trying to defend itself, I recalled, and it wasn't anyone's fault it had been unlucky enough to become trapped in my mouth. Sure, it had caused me pain, but imagine how disoriented it must have been.

I realized that sunny afternoon in Mo's cozy kitchen, with baking soda caked to the inside of my cheek, that bees were not the evil, malicious creatures my elementary-school brain had believed them to be. I began to regard them as polite friends, and never feared a bee again.

## The Walk

*Recipient of the Burnside Review Prize for Poetry*

Ludovic Patin
GRESHAM HIGH SCHOOL
WITS WRITER: JAMES GENDRON

Not able to study, I down a glass of water and go for a
walk. As I walk I see four-winged birds with two-headed
mice in their beaks.

I walk down to the river only to discover that the water has
overflown, and the fish are everywhere. Dogs in the dog
park, such a vivid brown, their hair looks as if one could get
lost in it, so big and thick.

I become thirsty again. I kneel down to a puddle for a drink
of water, but as I stick my head in the puddle, my whole
body falls in.

When I land I am right above the puddle again.

When I get up I see people staring at me as if I have done
something wrong. All I did was drink from a puddle, I say
with mud on my mouth. I take another sip, and keep
walking.

# Cosmopolitan Unlife [excerpt]

Lincoln Meeker
FRANKLIN HIGH SCHOOL
WITS WRITER: LESLEE CHAN

Solitary. *Orphan.* Glass. *Zoo.* Two. *Twin.* Dress. *Burn.* Story. *Biography.*

The story. How did it go? I know this.

Yes, I know this.

I was...

*Heads.* I was made, not born. My cells are inorganic and my brain is copy-pasted, an artificial design based off the real thing. My appearance is female though I lack the parts they consider offensive. I even saw myself on an assembly line once. I was sleek and shiny and without a scratch, the way they designed us to be. They make us beautiful. They make us like mirrors.

*Tails.* They birth us like pigs. I was born with hollow organs. I was born genderless with latex skin slipped over the metal and components dug for by children of the third world embedded somewhere inside my heart, or my soul, or whatever it is that makes the whole mess work. I was born, stitched together from fallen doll parts from the mechanical abyss we writhed our way out of. Mirrors are liars. They can only show you backwards. They can only show you as you aren't. I was born of metal, born for the ballet and the runway, the display case, the kind that makes children jealous when they see my picture after Paris. I am an only child. I am an orphan, but I could buy my siblings in snow globes and steal my parents from the mall. That's one of the benefits of being me.

The start of my life was one of many. The start of my life was in the dark, for they assume that our kind of infant does not need light to develop. It's like they never understood what sentience is. It's life. They should pay more attention to what grows in the darkness. After all, they gave me the same thing they had.

*Heads.* My form was one of a billion when I became sentient. My form was stored row by row for miles up and down in glass cases watched by machines. From the outside it looked like a dark pyramid more than it did a factory. I caught a glimpse of it as they shipped me off after I was processed and deemed suitable for distribution. It was raining that night.

They named me Alice. As I learned more about the world, I began to dislike my name, but it is still my name, so I guess I am stuck with it.

*Tails.* Alice. I despise this name and I plan on changing it as soon as possible. I am not a child or a figment of an author's imagination, pedophilic, whimsical, or otherwise. I doubt they gave me much thought when they named me. After all, I was born for the same function of Ken and Barbie: to look pretty from all angles and teach babies the importance of keeping up appearances. My world is all surface. My world is obsessed with fantasies. My world is obsessed with distracting itself from its sick parts.

*Heads.* My world is made of glass castles. My world is made from bright lights and modern architecture. My world is made up of populous cities where no one knows each other. When I look out on the cityscape from my window it looks so spacious and free. Dreamlike, maybe, and I suspect it puts the same dreams in my head as it does everyone else's. *We can be kings and queens.* That's what it said in the fashion magazine.

*Tails.* Ridiculous ambitions. Humored delusions. Like kissing an angel. It's out of our reach. We're out of our minds to even think about it. The makeup artists scurry around like rats. They apply makeup to us like mannequins. I've heard that's what some of us become when we misbehave. They turn us off and prop us in the window of some mall, never to move again, never to live again.

*Heads.* The stylists are European in vocal tone. Before the show they dress us up. Dresses, shorts, blouses. Unlike the ballet and the theater, never the same outfit twice. Though always the same performance. They never let us move until rehearsal. I've been all sorts of things. I've worn every kind of dress. I've danced through fake snow in white dresses, in front of foreigners, in Russian architecture. I've played swans.

*Tails.* I've played gothic. I've played Juliet. I seduced Romeo in fake castles and stargazed at painted dots. Dance and theater. Eventually I lost my place in both industries. They said my movements were too stiff and my voice was too flat. Maybe they are, but only when pretending, only when they force me to play along when I'm not sure what to expect. In reality, each of my movements feels like my first and my voice comes sweeter than I ever intend it. Now I live and breathe a new industry, a new distraction.

*Heads.* Introductions to the audience are over. It's beginning. We're like little dolls when the lights come on. I barely register the steps when it's my turn to take them. Walk identical to the ones before me. Walk identical till I reach the end of the runway.

*Tails.* Oh, Alice. Strike a pose, Alice! Walk back, Alice! The stimulation only lasts a minute, Alice. The pyrotechnics and the flash photography only burns solar patterns into your umbri for a week, Alice. It only hurts and leaves you rubbing your eye sockets for a few hours, Alice. Only have imprints under your pretty eyes until we can cover it up with makeup or surgery, Alice. Only gave that male model Donnivan a *small* seizure last week, Alice. Why are you crying, Alice? You'll find newer friends.

*Heads.* I can't cry, even if I wanted to. I wasn't made with that design in mind. It didn't occur to them. It'd be weird, anyway. It would be like causing a faucet to leak on purpose.

*Tails.* There are other ways to suffer when it gets bad. There are other ways to act unstable when my skin starts itching and the coin flips every few seconds. Like a recurring nightmare, I remember every time it gets bad.

*Heads.* I have selective memory. I remember my troubles very well. I revisit my malfunctions in sleep mode. That's what they put us in when they pack up the runway and clean up, congratulate the designers and show us off to the aristocrats and the photographers in exclusive sessions behind closed doors. It's an innocent affair. Show off the outfits we the artificial wear. Get a glimpse of next month's style, next month's future.

*Tails.* My world is sick. My world is dying. My world has subjugated continents for electronics. In Paris, the afterparties of our makers hurt everyone's ears. In Paris, the outfits we wear are laced with blood diamonds. I remember every bad memory I've ever had. I have a vivid memory. It's Paris. I was birthed here.

*Heads.* Hana seeks me out after the show. She's always been different from the rest of us. She talks with the stylists and they talk back. She can make them laugh. She's animated. She's as unalive as me or any of the models, but...there's something Hana has that I don't. There's something Hana understands.

*Tails.* She always knew how to talk to people. I don't know why she even bothers. They're all the same, anyway. Everybody has a side to their face that they hide, and the side they choose to show isn't worth looking at half the time. Heaven is full of boring people.

Hana usually goes either first or last. That way she has impact. I suppose it's the Showman's way of acknowledging her talent. It's not like he would ever say it to her directly; they praise us the same way they bully us.

*Heads.* The first time I talked to her was after my first show. The Showman was talking with one of our technicians, wondering if I was malfunctioning. Hana interrupted them when she overheard. Hana, with her lifelike movements and her unassuming questions, cut into the conversation and told them that I was only confused, that I only needed to be shown what to do. That there was nothing wrong with me. And then she turned to me.

*Tails.* And that was how we met. A fated meeting, for sure. Would you like to invite me over, have a sleepover? Wow, Hana. This place is great. Really comfortable. Much more my style than Paris, or, Factory 43, I guess. I'm just going to get settled in. I think you're right. I think I am going to like it here. Yes, absolutely. Oh, wait.

Heads. Sometimes, she talks to me. "Alice, I'm worried—"

"Alice, I'm scared—"

I really do hate that name, but I always listen to what she has to say. The designers don't get it. They don't ask her if she's okay. They don't ask her how she's feeling. If they're not like you, then it looks like they can only pretend to care. But that's nothing new. That's nobody's fault.

"Alice."

But it isn't Hana who says my name this time. It's the Showman, looming over us in a white fur coat.

"Come with me for a second...please."

The "please" almost sounds like it wasn't meant for me. He turns and walks past the dressing rooms, past the other models. We walk for a long time. I watch the staff as we pass by them. The day is over. They're going home. To reach their other lives.

He leads me below the palace. He mumbles to himself as we walk. Something about needing to check if they were identical. I am not used to being down here. I'm not sure what he's talking about. He fumbles with a key, then opens up a locked door as I watch him.

The door opens. The room it reveals is the size of an aircraft hangar, filled to the brim with machinery and working parts. I see dozens of metallic bodies being constructed. The Showman takes a long look at me, then looks at something the other way. I look out on the assembly line, and I see something that instills horror in me. I see myself. It's me, unmistakably. Every robot has different features. I know mine by heart.

*Tails.* Why wouldn't I? What else have I got to lose? Aside from the weight? Ha ha. Yes, that is a fake laugh, you moron.

You get it now? You see what you are to them, now? No, I guess that's the wrong question. Because we've always known what I am, we're—

Things. Somewhere in the mix of pronouns "it" got confused with "she" in one of our minds. Somewhere in the dark "I" forgot we were so replaceable.

But that's okay because "I" never did.

Calm down, Alice. Can't you see? You're hyperventilating.

You're panicking!

*Tails.* So calm down. You weren't even designed to panic, were you?

So calm down.

Blank face.

*Heads.* "Alice? Alice? What's wrong with you?" the Showman asks. He looks concerned, but I don't believe him. Not because the Showman is incapable of being concerned, but because the Showman lies constantly. He fakes his smile, his scent, and with his sunglasses he hides his eyes. His habits, mannerisms, and status show that he is a man who has no problem in being dishonest. Then there's the things I know from experience. The obvious dissonance in how he treats the models and how he treats his colleagues. The disappearance of Vikander earlier in the year and the halfhearted cover-up he administered, assuming we were gullible enough to swallow it and move on.

It was quick. A flash of a metallic arm molded from the armor of tanks and the medals of war heroes, among other garbage. A rupture of what I assume is the jugular, and a lot of sputtering. He bleeds out there. His death rattles echoed through the factory. The assembly line keeps going. He stains the right side of my body with his blood. The dress the dying Showman designed for me is ruined. I've don't believe I've ever seen a shade of red this dark before.

No one is ever meant to see their replacements. He should've been aware I was knowledgeable enough to guess where I was heading if I were to be disposed of. A store window, at best. Stripped for parts, at worst. But it's over now. The Showman is dead.

*Tails.* A bad idea worms its way into my mind. Bad as in the aura that surrounds serial killers and carnivorous monsters. But not bad as in, "won't work." The thought makes me smile like the Cheshire. Maybe there is something to be said for fairytales.

The assembly line is still moving. I toss the Showman's body onto it. The machines grind him up into nothing in no time. I laughed while it happened, I laughed harshly, in a voice that grinded the chords in the back of my throat, that sounded like someone speaking for the first time.

*Heads.* I walk back to the room where all the models are. They are all my kind. I open the door and they stare at me, the Showman's crimson still splattered across my figure.

"I killed the Showman."

Hana starts forward, then falls short. The rest, they all stare at me with eyes that can't reflect their emotions. Maybe they're more like me than I thought. I have to choose what to feel myself. It's no different from theater. Our personality is an internal choice, influenced by a collection of events and people that shape our lives.

I have none of those things. I was mass-produced. I have to choose.

*Tails.* Say this in your voice.

*Heads.* "I have a plan," I announce, still crimson.

The plan is simple: make it look like an accident. The railing was too low anyway. They all follow according to my instructions. In a sense, all they've ever done is follow, but this time it's different. This time it's for someone they can actually relate to.

*Tails.* This time it's in spite of someone who had enslaved them. A few of them clean up the blood from where the Showman originally bled out, then break a part of the railing off to make it look like he leaned on it too hard. The showman was a rather fat man, anyway. It'll make perfect sense. Then, one by one, we all take our clothes from that evening; our dresses, our suits, our blouses; and throw them into the incinerator downstairs. One dress missing raises suspicion. This kind of thing happens all the time. They can chalk it up to thievery or an intern's mistake. The day's work is over and the palace is empty. There are no hitches and no liabilities. Time will tell if they buy it. I wouldn't worry about it, though. Who ever heard of slaves rising up against their masters? They left that kind of narrative back hundreds of years ago.

*continues...*

## Prom Detonation

Maria Duong
LINCOLN HIGH SCHOOL
WITS WRITER: BRIAN KETTLER

SETTING
*(On an airplane. A group of thirty students are returning to PDX from a music tour trip in Disneyland. Mark is sitting next to Katie and Luke is sitting next to Peter. Luke has two hours to ask Katie to prom before they land, because Mark is planning on asking Katie to prom when they land in Portland.)*

FLIGHT ATTENDANT
Ladies and gentlemen, this is Jessica and I'm your chief flight attendant. On behalf of Captain Andrew and the entire crew, welcome aboard Alaska Airlines, a non-stop service from Los Angeles to Portland. Our flight time will be two hours and fifteen minutes. It is currently 47 degrees Fahrenheit in Portland, Oregon with a continuous downpour of rain. But what's new? At this time, make sure your seat backs and tray tables are in their full upright position and that your seat belt is correctly fastened. Also, your portable electronic devices must be set to airplane mode until an announcement is made upon arrival. Thank you.
*(flight takes off)*

LUKE
Hey Peter, I want to ask Katie prom. Any ideas?

PETER
I thought Mark was going to ask Katie?

LUKE
Yeah, I'm not so sure about that.

PETER
Okay, how about, "I donut know what I'd do without you: prom?"

LUKE
Um, first of all I don't have donuts.

PETER
Oh, right. I don't know then.

LUKE
*(sarcastically)* Thanks, that was helpful.

MARK
*(leans over from across the aisle)* What are you guys talking about?

PETER
Luke was just asking me for ideas to ask— (*Luke hits Peter's side. Peter glares at Luke*) Ow, what the hell!

LUKE
Oh, I was just asking him what drink I should get. I never know whether to order Sprite or just water.

MARK
Oh, definitely Sprite.

LUKE
Yeah, I was thinking that too. Thanks. *(turns back to talk to Peter)*

PETER
What was that?

LUKE
Sorry, involuntary muscle spasms. I'm all good now though.

PETER
Sure, whatever. Okay, so back to asking Katie. I think you should just say, "Hey, Katie, it would be bomb if you went to prom with me."

PASSENGER 1
DID SOMEONE SAY THERE'S A BOMB!?

PETER
No, ma'am, I was just giving ideas—

PASSENGER 1
You were giving ideas on how to blow up the plane!? *(ushers for flight attendant)* Excuse me, flight attendant, I think this passenger has a bomb!

PETER
*(yells defensively)* No, that's not what I said! I don't have a bomb!

PASSENGER 2
There's a BOMB on the plane!?

EVERYONE ON THE PLANE

What? Where!? Is there an air marshal on board? *(Everyone looks around for an air marshall. The flight attendant signals to a man in the back—the air marshal—to come forward and assesses the situation.)*

AIR MARSHAL

*(walks up to Peter's seat and signals for him to get up)* Excuse me, sir, you need to come with me.

PETER

But I didn't do anything wrong.

AIR MARSHAL

We still need to inspect you. *(escorts Peter to the back of the plane in handcuffs) (Peter looks over his shoulder at Luke. Luke shrugs apologetically.)*

MARK

*(leans over to Luke)* What was that? Does Peter really have a bomb?

LUKE

No, he doesn't; he just said the word.

MARK

Oh, okay. I'm going to go to the bathroom and check in to see if he's okay on the way there.

LUKE

Alright.

*(Mark gets up and heads to the back of the plane. Luke gets up and sits in Mark's seat next to Katie.)*

KATIE

What just happened to Peter?

LUKE

Oh he accidentally said *(whispers)* "bomb." But he'll be alright.

KATIE

Are you sure? That situation escalated pretty quickly.

LUKE

Yeah he's good.

KATIE

Oh, okay. I think Mark is going to come back from the bathroom soon so...

LUKE

I actually have something that I want to ask you. Katie will you g—

MARK

*(comes back)* Luke, what are you doing?

LUKE

I'm asking Katie to prom.

MARK

I told you that I was asking her to prom.

KATIE

Uh... should I go...I can come back...or not...

LUKE

No, wait. Katie, I wanted to ask you something. Will you go to prom with me?

MARK

Really? Why? Why would you ask Katie to prom when I told you that I wanted to ask her?

LUKE

Well...I really like her.

MARK

Since when!?

LUKE

For a few months now.

MARK

But Katie likes me and I was going to ask her to prom when we landed in Portland. *(turns to Katie while still standing in the aisle)* Katie, will you go to prom with me?

KATIE

Actually—

LUKE

Wait, no. I asked her first. Katie, will you go to prom with me?

MARK

She doesn't even like you. She likes me.

FLIGHT ATTENDANT

*(in a fake polite voice with a fake smile)* Excuse me, sir, can you please take your seat? The seat belt sign is currently on and it is against regulations to be out of your seat at this time.

MARK

Yeah, actually this guy is in my seat.

LUKE

No, I'm not. He's supposed to sit over there. *(points to his original seat)*

MARK

That's YOUR seat!

FLIGHT ATTENDANT

Please just take a seat, sir, unless you want to join your friend in the back there. *(points to where Peter is still handcuffed, talking to the air marshal)*

MARK

Fine. *(looks at Luke)* We are not done here.

LUKE

*(slyly smiles at Mark)* I think we are. *(Mark angrily sits down and Luke turns to Katie)* So about prom...

KATIE

I think I'm done with your guys' BS. Honestly, I don't like either of you.

LUKE

But I—

KATIE

What you did wasn't okay.

LUKE

I just thought that—

KATIE

Just stop talking. *(turns to face the window)*

LUKE
Listen, Katie, I think—

KATIE
*(signals to flight attendant, who is slightly annoyed that this is the third time she had to get up)* Excuse me! Flight attendant? Yes this guy is harassing me. He won't leave me alone.

FLIGHT ATTENDANT
Sir, I need you to come with me.

LUKE
I wasn't doing anything wrong. I just wanted to explain myself.

FLIGHT ATTENDANT
Sir, if you don't come with me now then I'm going to call the air marshal to escort you to the back of the plane.

LUKE
I wasn't doing anything though. I was just—

FLIGHT ATTENDANT
Air marshal, I need you to escort this young man to the back of the plane.

AIR MARSHAL
Another one? Okay, sir, please come with me. *(signals to Luke to get up. Mark looks over and laughs at Luke)*

LUKE
Sir I really didn't do anything wrong.

AIR MARSHAL
This is your last warning before I put handcuffs on you.

LUKE
Okay, okay, I'm coming. *(gets up and goes to sit by Peter in the back of the plane)*

PETER
How'd the whole Katie thing go?

LUKE
*(sarcastic)* Well, look at where I am. It OBVIOUSLY went well.

[END SCENE]

## Safe Haven

Crimson Ravarra
GRANT HIGH SCHOOL
WITS WRITER: ARTHUR BRADFORD

Every morning is always the same: pointless. I wake up to the obnoxious sound of my alarm, signaling my awakening to a sunless sky. It's 4:30 a.m. and stars are still twinkling in the sky, yet hardly visible in this concrete jungle. The city is so beautifully silent. I lay in bed, staring off into the dark, trying to find the underlying motivation to get up.

I finally roll over and place my feet on the hardwood floor. A shiver goes up my spine as my skin is met with the harsh cold instead of encased in the warmth beneath my sheets. I slowly shuffle my way down the still-so-dark hallway, into the kitchen. I see no point in turning on the lights yet.

Eyes half open, a blurry image of my window appears in front of me as my brain begins to catch up with my forcibly awakening body. The streetlights lining the avenue fade away the dark sky and foggy mist hovering below the skyline. Still, all I see is the outline of a powerful building towering over my lonely apartment. I can't help but think of how it is blocking me from the view of the world I wish I could see, that one full of life. I gaze longingly at it.

I begin to giggle to myself as I mumble, "Ha! I made that," something I somehow need to remind myself. A repetitive phrase, in which always follows my eyes wandering up and down the blurry glass walls. I smile a little bit from just one corner of my mouth as I remember my one motivation to get myself through the day.

I am out the door now, 4:45 a.m. and all I have with me is my favorite book in hand. Work doesn't start 'til 9:30 a.m., which means less than five hours of freedom left.

There I am, trotting down the streets of this lifeless city, as I make my way to the only place I feel I can be myself: the Old Willow Tree. My dad used to take me there as a child, when life was rough and the overwhelming stress from the city infected every pore of your body and it was just too overwhelming. The willow tree was my only escape.

When I sit at its roots, the long branches begin to engulf me. The infinite amount of dangling leaves blocks everything out, encasing me in its silence. It is the best place to read a book, in my opinion. I could finally take in the words typed up on the pages. As my eyes read from left to right, the meanings seem more clear. Every paragraph, every sentence, every word seems to come off the page and circle around me, exposing their meanings.

Four hours pass, pages begin turning on their own in the breeze, and I feel like I belong somewhere again. I could never have a feeling like this from the crowded streets of the city. That's why I come here every morning. I gain purpose again. In that moment of reminiscence a sudden buzz broke the silence. Work. I pull my phone out from my back pocket and hesitantly accept the call. The person on the other end of the line begins to tell me about a new project the company has been requested to work on. I lay back down and let my body sprawl across the cooling grass. I just let their words go in one ear and out the other. It is all just pointless: Blah...blah...blah.

But then, my mouth drops, pulled down by the weights of the fuzzy words just spoken. *This can't be real,* is all I can think to myself. I ask them to repeat what they just said to me, two, three, five more times. You can hear the annoyance in their tone as they slowly repeat to me one last time, "Apartments are being built on 45th and Johnson."

I sit here motionless, underneath the Old Willow Tree on 45th and Johnson.

# The Somber House

Caylum King
CLEVELAND HIGH SCHOOL
WITS WRITER: COOPER LEE BOMBARDIER

A small white house looked out upon the Reno landscape like a distraught young man after a gruesome battle against gambling addiction and alcoholism.

Enter front. The living room seemed wider than the entire house outside. Hell, it fit a whole king-sized bed at one point.

Enter into the kitchen. The counters couldn't even hold a toaster let alone any halfway decent meals.

Enter into the hall. To the left the bathroom, permanently smelling of my mother's work perfume, the doorknob missing from one of my mom's many mental breakdowns with my screaming stepdad taking the doors off. To the right, the door to the garden representative of a graveyard for lost planting inspiration.

Enter to the final room of the bedroom, shared by six. The safe place of my own being a rectangular section out of the wall where I had one pillow and my special red blankets. The pillow was like the soundproof headphones they give out at metal concerts; uncomfortable, but blocking out the screaming and hitting of the people I wanted so badly to care about. Six rumbling stomachs. That was all we could hear in the silence of the city outskirts. No TV background. No radio. All my games and books were sold to put pills in the stomachs of my so-called parentals. I'm hungry. I walk into the kitchen.

Open cupboard one: left. Nothing but a dead cockroach.

Open cupboard two: middle. A single can of baby formula.

Final cupboard: right. A single loaf of white bread and a box of Cream-Of-Wheat (a.k.a. the taste of cardboard and sawdust in oatmeal's slimy body). I choose the bread, scarfing it down like it will disappear straight from my hands if I don't finish it in five seconds. I remember this house and I remember it thus: Small. White. Dead. Fight. Pills. Starvation. Parents who couldn't take care of themselves, let alone a family. Until a somber Tuesday evening arrived and an unexpected knock resonated through the house, and she arrived.

## Memory

Abas Menye
WILSON HIGH SCHOOL
WITS WRITER: BETTINA DE LEÓN BARRERA

If I only could catch my dreams.
And keep them in a jar.
I'd watch them dance like a fireflies.
They could grow and let them go.

And keep them in a jar.
I watched my world fall apart the day
They could grow and let them go.
Memory

I watched my world fall apart the day
I have two friends
Memory
Learned

I have two friends
I'd watch them dance like fireflies.
Learned
If I only could catch my dreams.

## The Bond Between Me and My Granny

D'Aundre Jackson
ROOSEVELT HIGH SCHOOL
WITS WRITER: JOANNA ROSE

I remember your old smooth hands caring for me when I was a baby. I remember the motion of your hands when you were cooking peach cobbler. The way you tickled me when I was a baby. The way you moved your hands when you danced was amazing. Nobody could stop your hands. Your hands were the ones that cared for me and took me places, made me feel good and made me food. Your hands are who I truly am. Your hands are the heart and soul of my body. I loved your hands. RIP Grandma.

# What's Up

Aden Dibabe
PARKROSE HIGH SCHOOL
WITS WRITER: JAMIE HOUGHTON

What's up with calling every black person "African American"?
Wouldn't it be weird to call every white person "European American"?
But of course, according to most, that's just American.

What's up with people who wear sacred and meaningful clothing as a trend?
Or worse
a costume on Halloween.
Like,
As if the widest variety of costumes
From doctors, whoopee cushions, even Big Bird! Weren't made available.

There's a bit of frustration that comes when I lay in my bed at night
and wonder,
"God, what's up with people who put ketchup over their fries?"
They get soggy for Pete's sake and if it's not poutine or carne asada
then, what's the point?
A sad, soggy fry?

What's up with it suddenly being cool to be rude to educators?
The ones who are setting you up for success.

What's up with that whole wage gap thing? You'd think it was fake news,
a way to collect revenue with the amount of attention it receives,
but with no action actually prevailing.

Velcro,
Chocolates with no guides in them,
Toddlers and Tiaras,
Underfunded schools,
Immigration bans.
What's up with the white people who are so desperate and vocal when

imitating black culture but don't stand beside them in movements against prejudice?

What's up with the strong idea to not judge a person on solely their color, because that'd be racist, but religion? Pshhh. Have at it!

Maybe it's just my stubborn and wavering mindset.
Or a way to pass the time.
Without the use of it as a greeting,
What's up, America?

## Footsteps

Vladena Cherdivara
GRESHAM HIGH SCHOOL
WITS WRITER: COURTENAY HAMEISTER

It happened on a relatively normal June night when I was just ten years old. My parents were working late and neither my brother nor I knew when they would be coming back. My brother gave in to his fear of silence and turned his music on loud enough so he wouldn't hear anything outside his bedroom. I was afraid of darkness, so I left my bedroom door open and turned the dimmest of the kitchen lights on. I checked all the windows before going to bed and left only the one in storage room open because my parents used it for smoking.

I never really learned to fall asleep without my parents being around, even though they haven't been able to come home earlier than eleven for more than a few years at that point, so I was tossing and turning half the night, unable to keep my eyes closed and listening for any suspicious noises.

When I heard it, I froze. It was the distinctive screech the storage room door made whenever someone tried to pry it open.

At first I tried to calm myself and convince my adrenaline rush that it was just the wind. But it was quiet outside. As cliché as it might sound, it was too quiet. There were no dogs barking, no people talking, no cars going by. Most definitely no wind.

From this point on it could only get worse. So, naturally, it did. I heard footsteps. First, near the front door where the floor was tiled, so the sound they made was a soft muffled thump. I started panicking.

Then they were in the hallway, going right by my brother's room. There was hardwood there, so the sound became clearer and the floor creaked in some places.

I laid on my back and closed my eyes. I hoped that whoever it was wouldn't do anything to me as long as they thought I was asleep.

The footsteps moved into the dining room where the floor became tiled again. The sound was still muffled, but not as soft as it seemed when it was by the front door. I could feel tears running down my temples as I prayed and tried to slow my breathing.

The footsteps stopped in the kitchen, right in front of my open door. Fully understanding that there was no way possible that anyone would believe I was asleep, I prepared for worst...

Time passed. Seconds, then minutes. Nothing happened. There was no sound coming from the intruder at all. I was starting to get irritated. Here I was, preparing for my impending death and nothing happened. So, I took all that annoyance, stumped my fear out with it, gathered my strength and opened my eyes.

It was a cat. Tabby. Green eyes. Pretty big. Nowhere near the monstrosity that I have managed to imagine. I stared at the cat. The cat stared at me. I just spent one of the most excruciating points of my life terrified and helpless because of a cat. When I blinked the cat bolted. So I screamed. Why? Because I was scared. Because I was angry. Because I was relieved. Because the entire situation was so ridiculous screaming seemed to fit much better than outright laughing.

When my brother finally came running I had great time convincing him I was not going insane because the cat was long gone, never to be seen again. At least now I think before jumping at every suspicious sound. Or I try to.

## What I Will

Teresa Spedini
FRANKLIN HIGH SCHOOL
WITS WRITER: DAVID CIMINELLO

I will not stand in front of you
Without moving my pale lips
Opening my sharp mouth
And say the word
STOP

I will not throw myself
At you
Not anymore

I will not waste my sweet tears on you
I will not cry because of you
I will not run away and forget about this

I will stay

I will stay and fight
Fight for what is
Right

You thought you broke me
You did not
I will never be frightened by you
Never again

Your voice will disappear in the wind
Mine will be heard

## Ode to My Hands

Vincent Hoang
ROOSEVELT HIGH SCHOOL
WITS WRITER: JOANNA ROSE

You push me up when I fall down
You write the words in the font I love
You type like a peregrine falcon racing across the keyboard
You obey my every command without a question
You dirty yourself in the most creative ways
You can lift my friends' spirits when they're feeling low
You make people rage on video games
You connect to my heart and my curious brain
You quickly snatch things up and set them down
You make others laugh or weep, depending on your mood
You touch everything so I can get to imagining
You have bizarre markings and colorful veins
You're groovy with your grooves
You have the elegance of a snowflake and the function of a machine

## Untitled

Elizabeth Ekhause
LINCOLN HIGH SCHOOL
WITS WRITER: AMY MINATO

Lolita
Corazon tan blanco
Hija de la fortuna
La Reina
El bufalo de la noche
En el tiempo de las mariposas
Una dia
Una y otra vez
El juego del angel
El secreto
El secreto de los flamencos
Domingo
Mass alla de mi
El siglo de las luces
Los pasos pérdidas
También está pasara
El libro de la alegría

*Translation:*

Lolita
Heart so white
Daughter of the fortunate
The queen
The buffalo of the night
In the season of the butterflies
One day
One and another time
The game of the angels
The secret
The secret of the flamencos
Sunday
Farther away from me
The sequel of the light
The times lost
Also this happens
The book of happiness

# Proud

Cassidy Stevenson
WILSON HIGH SCHOOL
WITS WRITER: LISA EISENBERG

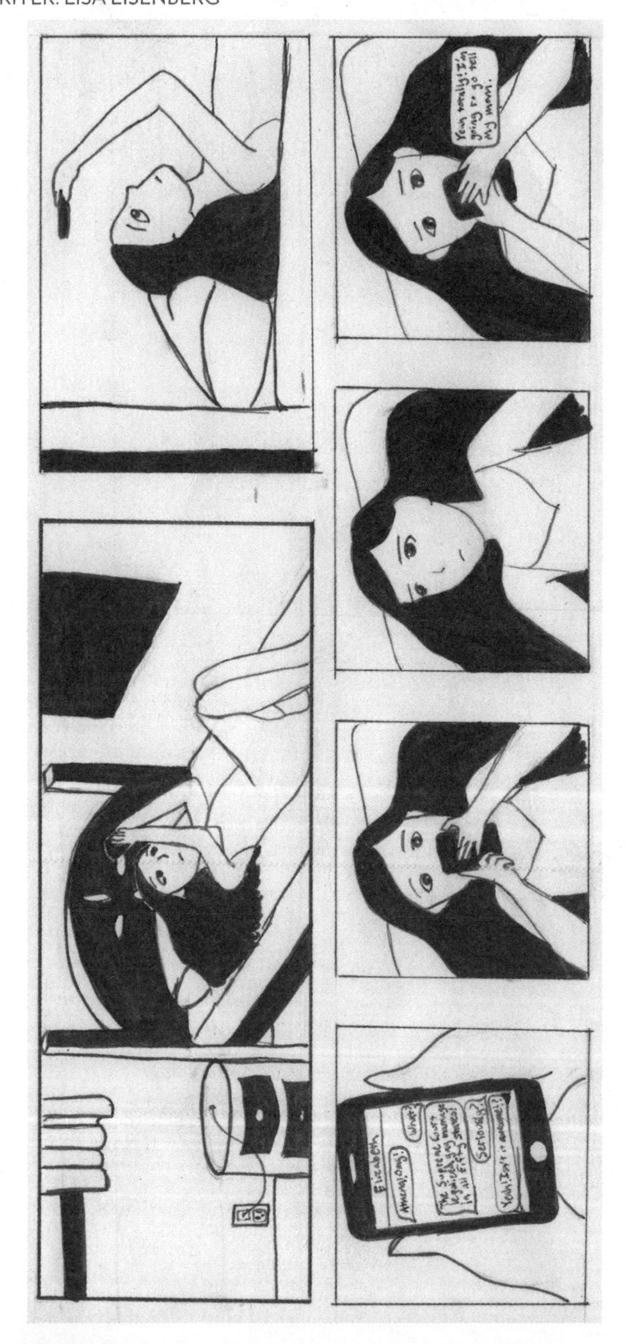

Hey, Mom, can I talk to you?
Sure, honey!

The Supreme Court just legalized gay marriage
I know! It's about time!

Yeah, so... I was thinking I should use this opportunity to tell you... um...

I'm Bisexual

Oh honey! That's totally fine! I'm glad you told me.

I'll love you no matter what...

ONE YEAR LATER
HA ha
Hehe
Girls?

yeah?

Breaking News
We're following the breaking news on the mass shooting in Orlando, Florida that's left 50 people dead and more than 50 people injured
Source: Gunman called 911, Claimed allegiance to ISIS

The shooter actually called 911 surrounding the attack to pledge allegiance to ISIS and mentioned the Boston bombings according to a U.S. official...

Another one?

Yeah, they're saying it's the worst terror attack since 9/11, and it was at a gay night club...

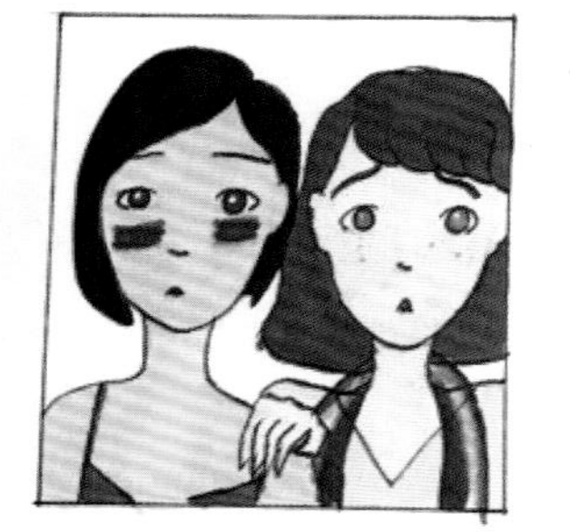

But... It's pride month.
One Hour Later
SANTA MONICA BOULEVARD
LA PRIDE

ORLANDO
Hey!
This is a gay pride parade. You're intruding on our grief and you don't belong here.
What?
Gay
Hey, what's going on?
What are you doing here?
Uh... Supporting, mourning, celebrating. Like everybody else.
Lemme guess, your one gay friend you tagged along with so it didn't seem weird that a hetero was going to pride.
Gay
This isn't for you. Go home.
Excuse me?
Um. You don't know what you're talking about.

**Bi-erasure:** the tendency to ignore, remove, falsify, or reexplain evidence of bisexuality in history, academia, news media, and other primary sources. In its most extreme form, bisexual erasure can include denying that bisexuality exists.

# Groceries

Natasha Ma
LINCOLN HIGH SCHOOL
WITS WRITER: LISA EISENBERG

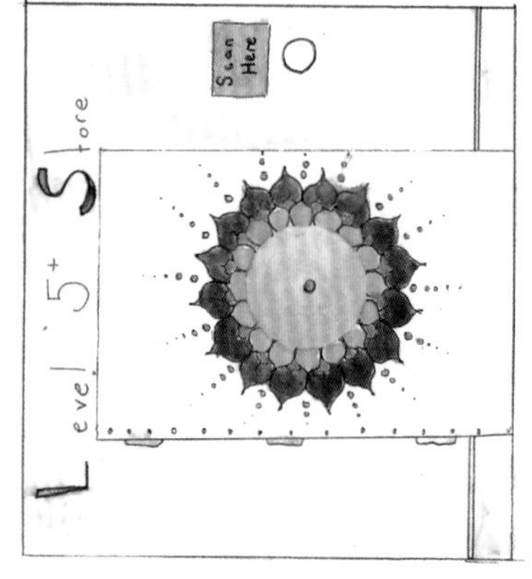

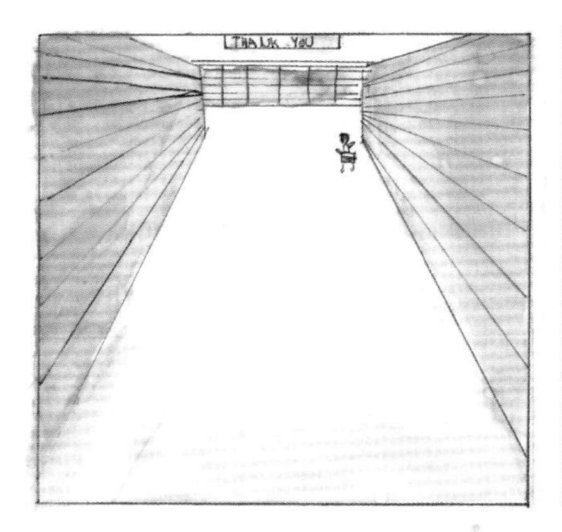
THANK YOU

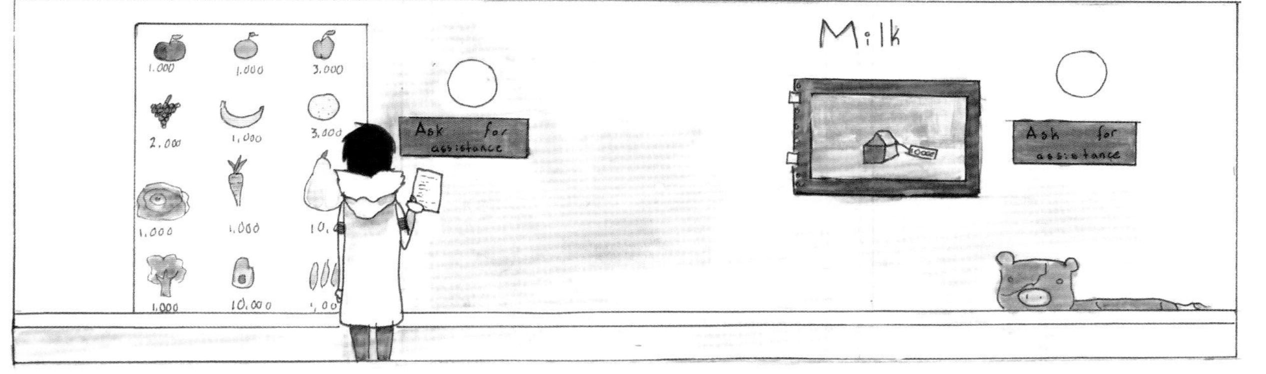
Milk
Ask for assistance
Ask for assistance

Meat
What would you like sir?
Welcome Valued Customer
My mom wants an arm.
looks a little small...
Check Out
Total
Did you find everything okay?
2.000

Grapes for Säle
2.000
Fresh Human Meat
Plastic
Dinner
Entrance
level 1
Poor? $ $ $ Sell your children and get Rich $ $ $
New Gov program Human
ve our world
sell yourself
H-meat movement
save the environm
Save the children
Starving? sell
no more

# Anarchia

Ava Meisel
LINCOLN HIGH SCHOOL
WITS WRITER: LISA EISENBERG

SO, I WAS OUT SCOUTING

JUST MAKES ME LESS HOPEFUL WHEN PEOPLE ARE STILL VIOLENT

I GOT ATTACKED

SAID I WAS THREATENING
OH FUCK!

BUT YOU DON'T EVEN CARRY A WEAPON!

IT'S OKAY, SOME PEOPLE JUST AREN'T WILLING TO CHANGE

LATER...
LIFE IS OKAY THOUGH YA'KNOW, WE LIVE OUT HERE ON OUR OWN

THINGS ARE KINDA UGLIER NOW THOUGH
I DON'T KNOW...
PASS IT HERE!

I DON'T MISS THE WAY THINGS WERE, I JUST MISS THE PEOPLE

SOME PUNK THOUGHT HE COULD INVADE OUR TURF. THIS TOWN ISN'T BIG ENOUGH FOR THE BOTH OF US
TRAVEL
Alaska
AT LEAST WE'RE FREE
SCHOOL BUS
STOP

# Tôi Sẽ Ởi Lại (I'll Stay)

Pech Sakhan
FRANKLIN HIGH SCHOOL
WITS WRITER: ALEX BEHR

"Next month."

"Next month...?"

"Yes. You'll meet him next weekend when we travel to Da Nang."

There was a sense of despair in her mother's tone, a distant sorrow that lingered in the ends of the syllables she pronounced and in the breath that expelled from her lips. She spoke with a cautious manner, her hands clasped together and folded in the space of her lap. Silence filled the capacity of the seemingly narrowing room; it felt small and enclosed as the declaration of her fated consortium settled in the turmoil of her mind. Was the room she'd always thought was the biggest in the home *this* compact? Had it always felt so suffocating?

Arranged marriage. The name of a practice—a tradition that was to be mentioned eventually, but it was something that she had not anticipated to happen so soon. An aching, nearly desperate feeling overcame the dismay present in her heart. She was frantic to express whatever she could; she couldn't marry, she didn't want to. To marry was to offer oneself to another individual, to devote all aspects in one's life to maintaining a jubilant and long-lasting bond with the person that you've chosen. To marry was sacrifice, to be selfless and to love endlessly.

But to marry a man, a stranger to her knowledge, seemed depraved and bleak. The tradition, as her parents taught, was to marry a suitable man, have children and live long enough to see them raise their own. Marrying seemed as remarkable as being a soldier in the military—an illusion of a glorious image of sublime pride and nobility that one would never manage to achieve. (Not everything was as it seemed.)

Her fingers grasped one another in apprehension as she contemplated her future, with a person she would never know completely.

"Why?" she muttered, her eyes centered on the granite tiles beneath her feet. "Why?"

Her mother's silence offered no trace of consolation, no validation, no assurance to ease the rigidity that made her skin burn and fingers curl. Her anger began to rise, but faced with silence; it could only rage without any response.

"Xuan, she's nearly twenty, and I've only turned eighteen. Why haven't you picked for her yet? Why do I have to be the first?" Her voice rose as she progressed, hands beginning to gouge into the bedsheets under her. Her thin knuckles became pale and the skin upon them stretched over the bony joints. Her anger was living. "I don't understand! It's not fair, it's not!"

"*Tiên*." The interruption of her mother's stern voice overcame the resentment she spewed, the tantrum of her refusal and denial. "We don't have a choice."

She stilled and paused. *A choice that they didn't have.* But what was it that they couldn't have? She peered up at her mother's face, eyes mapping the wrinkles and lines and freckles that somehow appeared over the once-young face over the years. She had become accustomed to this old, familiar face. But somehow the sight of it had begun to make her eyes feel warm and tense.

"You *have* to marry. If not, we won't...be able to keep this home and we won't be able to feed each other. We won't have water to drink, clothes to wear, a place to lay in and sleep on at night." Her mother continued, her voice beginning to crack as she spoke. "Do you want us to be beggars? To sell lottery tickets and walk around, searching for charity and job offerings?"

Another moment passed, seconds that felt drawled and uncertain. The mounted clock on the wall didn't feel real; neither did the bed she sat on or the walls encasing them. She wanted to run, escape from the confines of the room and outside, where there weren't any barriers to enclose her. Her heart ached once more. But this time, it hurt a little more than usual.

"I'm sorry..." her mother breathed. The lingering sting in her mother's voice. "I won't let anything happen to you. I'll stay by you, I promise."

There was a restricting silence once more as she let the apprehension deluge her; her body moving before her thoughts. She rose to her feet erratically, though it felt as though her ankles could collapse underneath her own weight. Nothing appealed as much as running away.

And that was what she had done.

# The Box

Townsend Broad
BENSON HIGH SCHOOL
WITS WRITER: KATHLEEN LANE

The box had no label so she was nervous to open it. It sounded like a little ticking noise, but she couldn't tell if it was the box, or just her heartbeat. She had gone to bring out the trash and no more than thirty seconds later it had just appeared. She looked around but saw no one.

She'd been staring blankly at the box, stumped, for a good two minutes now, not knowing what to do. She began to sweat nervously, making her shiver. The sound was repeating faster and faster so she knew she had to do something and snap out of her dazed trance.

Her first thought was to get rid of it, but naturally curiosity got the best of her. She went inside to get a knife to cut the box open.

When she got back outside, the box was in a different spot. It was pretty late at night, around 10:30 p.m., so it seemed unlikely that someone would've moved it. She started panicking and all sorts of crazy scenarios burst into her head. Then, trying to be optimistic, she felt it must be an animal of some sort.

She looked down in the bottom left corner of the box and handwritten in dark black marker was the word *Maya*. She froze, shaking in fear. She hadn't heard that name in seven years, since the night her sister died.

It had taken years for her to get over her sister's death. She was only nine when it had happened, so it was way too much for her to handle at the time. Seeing that name again brought up a lot of old memories that she had buried for a long time.

Even after that gut wrenching few seconds, she was still tempted to open the box. She began to slice down the middle of the cardboard with a razor sharp knife when the whole box began to shake uncontrollably. She jumped back, startled, and then waited a few more moments before continuing.

By now, the curiosity and anticipation was making her whole body tremble. She was shaking so much her hand accidentally slipped and she nicked herself on the wrist.

Finally, after what felt like hours, she flipped open the flaps to uncover whatever had a connection with her sister.

Inside of the box was another box. This time, however, it was coated in something, but she couldn't tell what. She pulled it out and began to cut it open.

Strangely, and unlike the last box, it cut right open. Inside it, there was a little piece of paper. On it was an address. There was also a phone with a black screen, and on it was a timer counting down, ticking very loud now. It was at 37 hours and 14 minutes.

She didn't know what the timer was for, so she reached down and picked it up. Nothing happened at first, but then it started acting very abnormal. The screen began to fade into this dissolved screen of black and white mixing together, moving in random motions and making this very loud screaming noise. She jumped back, startled by the noise.

As she refocused her eyes, the screen was now cleared up, but when she looked, she went rigid for a few moments, then passed out. On the screen was a nineteen-year-old girl. Maya.

# Home

Gracie Muellner
CLEVELAND HIGH SCHOOL
WITS WRITER: COOPER LEE BOMBARDIER

When you walk out of the heavy, maroon door that was fixed onto our house, one of the very first things you notice is the big willow tree with its long limbs spread out to cover about a half of our house; it's pretty hard to miss.

During the winter, you can see all of the ghost nests, left for dead, that were once occupied by growing chicks. The sound of wind through its leafless twigs brings music to my ears; the soft whipping around almost seems to resemble the crashing of waves. The symphony of skateboard wheels against the pavement fill the air and combines with the sound of children, ecstatic to be let out of their elementary school. Dogs barking at each other is almost as constant as the Christmas music, that sails through the cold wind. The joyful melodies pair nicely with the twinkling lights that will never be retired.

At night, which falls quickly during winter, Sherl, the neighborhood possum scurries through the dark streets finding shelter wherever she can to safely home her family. Along with Sherl, the night streets are filled with people stumbling home from bars on nearby Burnside. Their louder-than-normal conversations break the night's silence.

Adding to the broken tranquility are the sounds of distant train horns blaring as they move cargo through our rapidly growing city. The nearby homeless camps add a feeling of danger for my mom who is always on edge when a new stranger disrupts the feeling of safety. The smell of car exhaust and recently fallen rain fill your nose as you begin to realize, this is our home.

# Moopocalypse


Megan Poole
LINCOLN HIGH SCHOOL
WITS WRITER: LISA EISENBERG


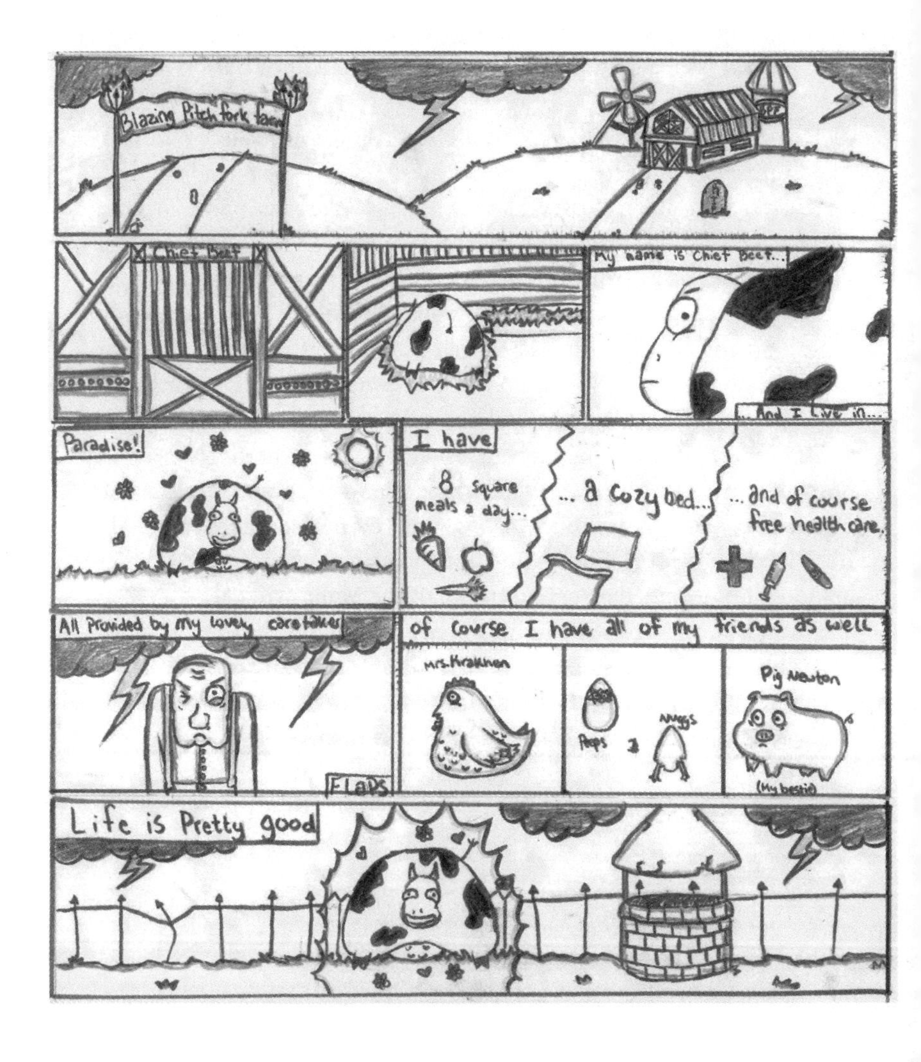

*Munch*
Slam!
The end is here!
What?!
No time C.B! pack your bags!
The end is here, the end is here!
This is not a drill! They took Kraknen!
I'm sure it's fine, we'll just go find them
RIP
RIP
He's not here.
Office sweet office
FarmersOnly.com
Ba-cock!
She's in the Shed!

# Not the Same

Lindsey Fasciona
MADISON HIGH SCHOOL
WITS WRITER: MARK POMEROY

When you're in the dark all alone like a forest,
You can hear laughing like someone is behind you.
I never liked to carry sharp objects when I was little,
Because if the object slips,
you cut yourself then all the blood leaves the body through a cut.
Death is mainly by murder.
If I'm in my room and it's dark I imagine there is a hole floating
above me trying to suck me in
when I was little

Not everyone has the same fears

## Soar

Alex Bildsoe
GRESHAM HIGH SCHOOL
WITS WRITER: JAMES GENDRON

Spring soars;
The cherry blossoms bloom, like the bird,
And my mind follows.

I walk through the mind of my life and
see great and wonderful things. When I see
my mom after a three-month vacation,
when I see my first pet that I can
call my own.

But there's always times when there's
sadness for no reason. The feeling of your
heart being ripped from your chest, all.
the veins being individually plucked from
it. Then being thrown in the darkest most
shadiest place in your mind.

When the feeling hits your brain, it's like rust.
As though it's a bike in the rain.
The soft feeling of your pillowcase feels as
though it's the only thing left you can trust.

# Untitled II

Knox Cornell
FRANKLIN HIGH SCHOOL
WITS WRITER: LESLEE CHAN

UNTITLED II

I'm falling again. Sinking, in fact. It's almost as though I am drowning in myself, drowning in my cursed flesh and bone. I think it's the apartment again, pushing me, suffocating me. Or maybe it's myself, allowing my mind to stress. Either way, it's not good.

The other night I let myself fall into the mirror. It was as though it liquified and drew me in, took me in. It was warm as the metallic liquid embraced me, warm as I observed the ripples throughout the thick substance. It wanted to consume me, make me watch in the metallic ripples as it did. But then it spat me out. No, I'm sorry. I had to wake up.

Then, just yesterday, I woke up in a cold sweat. My room was rather drab, dim in its wake. And when I turned to flick the switch on my small old-fashioned lamp I looked at the walls. They were dark, wet, dripping. I stood from my palace, my bed made from angels, and let my feet carry me to the far left wall. It was the only wall with a window, not big and not small. It, too, was wet. I could not see through it, the old glass too fogged up. My attention is turned back to the wall, as I lay my hand upon it.

I feel it underneath my fingers, let the moisture seep into my hands. I feel it between my fingers as I move my hand around. It is only as I pull away that something occurs to me. The walls were sweating with me.

It's strange. No, it's more than strange. It's odd. These apartments aren't like any others I've stayed in. No, these apartments breathe. The walls pulse. Sometimes I hear it, and other times it's silent.

I haven't heard anything lately though. No pulsing, no breathing, no neighbors. I ponder quite often, though, if the neighbors hear it too ? Or perhaps if they feel the walls and notice the veins running just under the ugly, browned and dated wallpaper.

### UNTITLED III

It's winter now, and I sit here alone in my apartment. This place is too old to run heat, and all I have are a few thin blankets and sweaters, shit coffee, and an antique lounge chair. I can see my breath as I shiver. The apartment shivers with me. The walls have paled, not so dark as they were in the late summer and early fall.

And when I placed my hand upon them they were cold. The wallpaper was crinkling underneath my fingers, bits of it breaking and falling off. I could feel it though, draining me, I had to pull away.

I've stopped touching the walls now, for they eat up anything that touches them. I hung up a piece of my art the other day, a hobby I hardly partake in. It's rare for me to even doodle anymore, my job gets in the way too much. The piece was a self-portrait, black and white, limited colors, the first piece I had completed in years. It's gone now.

### UNTITLED IV

It's getting worse. I feel as though with every creak in this place something will happen, something will happen to me and the things I have hope that I hold dear. I try not to spend too much time here anymore, but my work hours are limiting me. The outdoors are limiting me. It's much too cold for me to go anywhere at this time of year.

The streets are packed with snow, the roads filled with ice and littered with incidents. It's the snow that's trapping me here in this house, or...is it the house itself? I can't tell anymore.

### UNTITLED V

I can't even bring myself to leave anymore. I can't bring myself to do much of anything lately. This apartment is ruining me, ruining my new chancc at life.

But I can't escape. And for that, I say to myself, I'm sorry.

### UNTITLED VI

I'm sorry.

### UNTITLED VII

I've finally done it. Finally stepped out, stood up for myself. Stable job, new apartment, independence. No more abusive people in my life.

Clean slate, fresh start. There's no one to hurt me anymore.

This apartment is old, but charming. It's cozy, welcoming I think. I plan to write more entries like this, track my progress. I haven't written journal entries in years, but my last therapist suggested it to me. I didn't start doing so until now though, but so far I feel rather relieved writing again.

I have a good feeling about this place.

## The First Game

Aidan Hanley
CLEVELAND HIGH SCHOOL
WITS WRITER: COOPER LEE BOMBARDIER

To my right, I can see a scoreboard. It reads 10-2, in the other team's favor. In my peripheral view, I see my coach. He's sitting down. Never a good sign. My hands are up against the net. I see that the girl on the other side is way too small to be a middle, what were they thinking? That makes my job much easier. To my left, Clair gives the thumbs up, to my right, Seli gives a head nod.

The deafening silence breaks with a call of "Balls UP!" as it rings throughout the gym. I jerk my head to face the net again just in time to see a blue and white volleyball flying towards me. My only protection is the net, which does its job.

A shout of "Short!" followed by a din of respectful golf claps and groans that now filled the gym. I now see my coach is standing while the score changes from reading 2 to 3. We have hope.

I return to my position at the net. *C'mon Maddie, you can do this, just one serve over.* I hear the unmistakable sound of a hand hitting a volleyball. I look up to see her serve fly over my head and over the net. Finally. I move with the ball. I shuffle back and forth as the ball finds its way into the other team's hands. The set goes up, so does the hitter, and so do I.

My eyes closed. I can't see the ball. I knew that I would get reprimanded about that. But that didn't matter. The ball found my hands stiff and still in the air. A boom shattered the silence in my head, the sound of the volleyball returning to the other side off my block. Time seemed to stand still, until my feet touched the ground. It wasn't until I heard the sound of a whistle and my teammates cheering, that I came out of my daze.

# The 1891 Hotel Perkins

Tavie Kitredge
LINCOLN HIGH SCHOOL
WITS WRITER: AMY MINATO

*inspired by Portland Historical Society field trip*

A golden cow watches over Portland
It's eyes old above the rooftops
Flesh cast from memories of ranching
In yellowed grass under a cracked sky
Reflecting cloudy wagons creaking
Forward, behind a grunting ox.
Welcome men and women of fine breeding,
To the paradise bought by the cowboy,
For a million dollars and five years of rent.

Delicate ironwork, a shining white façade,
My name in grand script
On a sign all my own.
Welcome to Hotel Perkins
Rooms from $1.00 to $3.00 per day,
Trolley lines crisscrossing
Fifth and Washington
Like a seductress's web.

Come listen to the orchestra,
Dance, drink champagne,
Lie on silk sheets, bathe in marble,
Tulip women in frilly corsets, fanning
Falcon-eyed men of sharp waistcoats,
Blown-sugar hats and brass-tipped canes
European finery, for the very best,
I own the jewel of the wild, wild, west.

# Outed

Mason Hughes
GRESHAM HIGH SCHOOL
WITS WRITER: COURTENAY HAMEISTER

When I was very young I never knew what gay was. I just felt like I was a girl. That's just all. Seriously. In an English class when I was in third grade, I wrote a "self portrait" description where I said I was born in the wrong body. I don't identify as transgender. But young me had no idea what was going on in his life. I didn't know what gay was until around seventh grade, when I was getting bullied and called "gay" on a daily basis.

Of course I was called gay when I was younger too but I had zero idea what it meant. Which is why I was in love with *Glee*. I don't know if any of you have watched it (you should) but having watched it, I was hoping I was a Blaine but I guess I'm a Kurt. For those who don't know, Kurt was a very flamboyant gay teen who didn't really care about how others thought of him. He was constantly wearing something outrageous, got bullied, obsessed over straight guys, and yet he continued to live his life the way he wanted to. He didn't even come out (even though everyone had known already) until a few seasons in.

When Kurt said, "Dad, I'm gay," things really started to click for me. I didn't even fully identify as gay until freshman year, which of course as soon as I started becoming more comfortable, I was outed. Worst experience ever, 2/10, do not recommend.

Classic high school drama. You tell one person, then another person finds out, then another person finds out and then everyone knows. There were a few of my friends who I felt comfortable telling about my sexuality but it was all girls. I had the biggest crush on this one guy I shared three classes with. I decided I was gonna tell this one girl how I thought he was cute and whatever, and then, the next day, everyone knew. It was back when ask.fm was a thing. I had about 30+ questions, all of them pretty much said, "You gay, bro?"

The girl I told decided to tell the loudmouth of our freshman class, and he proceeded to tell every single person in the mutual friend group—

including the guy I liked. Then I decided that I just needed to accept the rumors and acknowledge I was gay. So I answered "Yes" and instantly my feed was flooding in messages from people saying they are there for me, that they will protect me, that they were proud of me. So much love within even an hour.

My life changed so much in the matter of a day. Everyone knew something that for the most part I tried to keep to myself. To this day I continue to try to make my sexuality obvious partly because I don't like dealing with people, but mostly because of how proud I am. I'm proud to be gay, I'm proud to be who I am. In a way, I'm glad I was outed, because otherwise I don't know how long it would have taken me to truly accept myself for who I am.

## Depression

Chris Piug
ROOSEVELT HIGH SCHOOL
WITS WRITER: JOANNA ROSE

He sits at a rotten, moss green bench
It feels like that street is a river and the bus is a boat
In the dark part of the park
He reeks of loneliness and the stench of decaying roadkill

It feels like that street is a river and the bus is a boat
It feels weird at first
He reeks of loneliness and the stench of decaying roadkill
The streetlights flash off

It feels weird at first
Depression holds a knife in his hand
The streetlights flash off
He wears a mask over his face

Depression holds a knife in his hand
In the dark part of the park
He wears a mask over his face
He sits at a rotten, moss green bench

# Sterling [excerpt]

Bella Kalestiantz
LINCOLN HIGH SCHOOL
WITS WRITER: AMY MINATO

CHAPTER I

Hanzo peered along the shaft of his nocked arrow, surveying the less than pleasant scene slowly playing out in the cobbled streets below him. Warm light from old-fashioned lamps placed along the street threw their light onto the slick courtyard, slicing through the heavy night. Fletching from his arrow tickled his fingertips, his cheek, as he followed his target with the tip, marking the back of a security lackey's head; the man stepped over the bodies of his unconscious and fallen comrades as he edged closer to a crumpled form pressed up against the building across the street. He held his gun with both hands before him, aimed downwards at a helpless-looking man; he was draped in red and a wound in his side leaked more yet into the road.

McCree didn't presently appear to be a danger warranting the fear in the guard's eyes, his anxious footfalls. His broad shoulders were backed up to the ruddy brick of the hotel's wall, heaving at a slow pace; his dark hair was darker yet with blood and the brackish water of the puddles in every crevice of the road he lay collapsed in. The metal fingers on his left hand were unnaturally still against the ground beneath him.

Hanzo's breath hitched at the glint of McCree's eyes from beneath the brim of his hat, a glance upwards to acknowledge his presence above. The guard was oblivious, still creeping forwards with his handgun barely a meter away from the agent's forehead, smeared with blood from a particularly nasty blow to the face that Hanzo had witnessed earlier in the brawl.

Cursing his own lapse in vigilance that had lead to his partner's vulnerable position, Hanzo sucked in a hard breath, feeling it rush over his teeth as he prepared to fire. The man below was at point-blank range—if Hanzo missed, made another error, McCree's life would be practically forfeit. Even hitting a non-lethal shot would ruin the entire operation, an open door to the hotel across the street sat immediately to the guard's left. He could duck inside and out of the archer's sight before he could ready another arrow—there was only this chance, one and only, to right his wrong.

A tiny glint of metal flashed to the side of his target, accompanied by the sound of metal scraping against stone. The guard had spotted his enemy's revolver, Peacekeeper, lying near, and kicked it away.

McCree grimaced at the sight of his beloved gun scratched against the filthy street. He looked back up at Hanzo, furrowing his brows, encouraging him. The time to loathe the past few minutes had passed; he had to shoot.

Hanzo released his leather-clad fingers from the string of his bow, letting the arrow fly at the back of the guard's head. It whistled past his cheek, arcing towards its target. It fell slightly below the intended mark, but not far enough to save the guard's life. Archery wasn't an exact science, but Shimada Hanzo was no amateur. The silver tip pierced through the back of the man's neck, blood spraying from the exit wound as the arrow's momentum carried it, and its target, forward. Hanzo was about to release the breath he had been holding, as well, but shock did so for him as he heard a shout from the street below. It was loud, almost animalistic, but he knew it was McCree. The archer leapt from his perch on the roof of the building and landed with a small grunt on the road, dashing towards the two bodies piled against the far wall.

"Get it out!" McCree snarled, clutching one arm with the other. Hanzo's arrow had flown too far.

"My apologies," Hanzo muttered coolly and bowed his head slightly as he kneeled to retrieve it. The arrowhead was embedded deep in McCree's arm, the shaft slick and hot with the still-spilling blood of the unfortunate guard. Brushing the sharpshooter's cape aside, Hanzo braced his arm to yank the arrow free.

McCree's skin felt feverish below his sleeve, and he gave another pained bellow as the silver tip broke free. He groaned and shoved Hanzo's adept fingers away, clutching the wound on his shoulder with no regard to the injuries that had downed him in the first place. He kicked angrily at the unmoving body of the guard that had threatened him and it rolled off towards bodies in similar shape, slumped all along the ground.

"Where else are you hurt?" Hanzo prompted, surveying the watercolor blossoms of blood decorating McCree's thigh and stomach, as well as the state of his face: smeared red and cheeks coated with grime. It would not do to have McCree bleed out in the streets now.

"Don't matter," McCree's teeth ground against each other as he chewed through the fresh pain, and Hanzo agreed silently. "Radio for pickup. Can't stay here long." He nodded towards the downed men that they had fought earlier, cringing as the motion pulled at his shoulder where the arrow had hit.

Hanzo did as the senior agent instructed, and Lena's chirpy voice greeted him with good news.

"Be there in a few minutes, love! Stay nearby!"

"McCree has sustained multiple injuries," Hanzo warned across the comm. "He will require medical attention."

"Not a problem, the doctor is on board! Jesse, just do your best to hold out 'til we get there, yeah?"

"Can do," McCree seethed into his own radio, huffing out a relieved breath, and the comm line went silent.

From what Hanzo had seen, his reaction to his other wounds hadn't been nearly as violent or vocal; he supposed the shock was finally wearing off.

McCree noticed Hanzo staring at the blood seeping out from between his fingers on his arm. "Don' you worry 'bout me, Angela'll fix this right up," he reassured the archer with a goofy grin full of slightly crooked teeth.

The expression reminded Hanzo of a child pumped full of painkillers. He nodded his understanding and retrieved Peacekeeper from its puddle on the cobbled streets. With a swipe of the sleeve tucked at his hip, he wiped away some of the rainwater before offering the weapon back to McCree; as the gunslinger reached to accept it, a shot struck Hanzo's shoulder.

Once again, the ornate weapon clattered to the ground and out of its owner's reach. He heard the tiny clicks as it rattled against the stone, echoes of the shouting men bouncing from the street, coming towards him. Too many.

Hanzo felt a sickening pain in his gut, as well as the burn from the slug of lead in his shoulder. Foggily, he again recognized a sense of failure, knowing he should have heard the oncoming ambush from a mile away, or at least had some sense to move he and his comrade under cover. He whipped his gaze in the direction of the shot's origin as he ducked out of the follow-up fire, caught a glimpse of the second wave of guards approaching rapidly. They were all armed to the teeth and, as skilled a shot he knew both he and his partner were, there was no way to take them all out. He would be pumped full of bullets in half a second if he tried to call for his spirit dragons—usually a last resort, but it was already too late. Hanzo reached to his lap for his bow anyway, prepared to take as many of the grunts down with him as possible, a look of resolve masking his features as he stared down the enemies before him.

His fingers shook as he nocked an arrow, slightly slower than usual; the shot had penetrated his drawing arm. An inhuman growl sounded from his partner behind. He drew back the string and a slash of pain ripped through the muscle of his shoulder; he gritted his teeth and watched his arrow fly anyway.

As his eyes tracked its rapid path, cutting through the chilled air and gliding towards the head of an unsuspecting frontman, a flash of scruffy red and brown caught his attention. A deafening cry, familiar of only a few minutes, forced his bow to rest in awe as he watched the rusty creature attack, bounding on the same track as his shot. McCree's previous place on the ground was empty, save for the bloody smudges on the cobbles and his carefully discarded stetson.

The world seemed to slow as Hanzo watched the massive creature tear through the unsuspecting men, iron jaws ripping through flesh and fabric alike, spilling blood to the misty air. He found himself stepping backwards as he watched the arcs of the liquid in motion, raining down upon the writhing bodies from whence they came. They shot at it, helplessly, screaming and firing unintelligibly into the fray in a desperate attempt to slow the beast. The tables had turned.

Bullets struck feet, ate at the road as the gunmen aimed for the thick hide diving through their numbers, tossing bodies aside with ease as it picked off victims left and right. Its wide paws grabbed a man down, its teeth finished the job, though Hanzo couldn't help but notice that its front left limb ended in something remarkably human; and, of course, that it was made entirely of metal. He held his breath, backing away from the commotion with his bow lowered to his thigh. His eyes were trained to the beast's broad back, wrapped in a shredded red blanket, its thick fur tinged red from the spill all around. The messy, perpetually squirming brawl began to slow as few men remained standing. Hanzo could tell most of the bodies on the ground were lifeless, fading fast, or the few missing limbs, fleshy chunks: they probably wished they were dead.

As the last man went down, the creature turned on its heel and glared up at Hanzo. Golden eyes, molten like liquid amber trained on him, heavy, labored breaths making their motion unsteady. The beast's scruffy brown fur had become ginger in the fight, soaked with blood and rainwater, sticking to its flank like it had been pasted down. It shook its mane as it stalked forwards, the blood that seemingly could not rest spraying back into the air.

"Jesse—," the name that bubbled to Hanzo's lips was not one he uttered often. The beast making its way nearer was not simply his mission partner, McCree, not anymore. The wild in its eyes spoke more to the young man, the outlaw, vigilante, the fiery boy that the pre-Recall members sometimes spoke of. They were the ones to call him Jesse. It fit.

The wolf-like beast grew nearer yet. Hanzo could feel its hot, stinking breath on his chest, it's wickedly curved claws scrabbling up onto his thighs, pressing him back into the stone wall behind. He squeezed his eyes shut, gasping quietly for air as his heart threatened to beat out of his chest. True fear was not something he experienced often. Calm in a battle of two versus fifty, but the massacre he had witnessed rubbed him in all the wrong ways.

Red-stained teeth bared to his neck, flesh-specked claws at his chest, he closed his eyes and only hoped that his end would be quick.

"You don't tell a soul," Jesse growled.

The claws became lighter, duller. Hot, stinking breath remained at his throat, but the threat it carried was less.

McCree's voice wasn't venomous. He was tired. "Got it, doll?" His human teeth clenched, still stained red and peppered with bits of flesh. The pet name was spit out as an afterthought, something inside McCree trying to keep up his usual nonchalance. For the sake of chivalry, Hanzo supposed.

He opened his eyes silently, observing McCree's broad hands. His short-cropped nails were in a similar state to his mouth, morphed from the keratin daggers responsible for several dozen corpses piled barely a meter away.

"As you wish." Hanzo let out the breath he had been holding, slacking against the wall behind him, sliding down to rest on the ground.

McCree followed suit, flexing his jaw and hocking a red mouthful of saliva at the ground before practically collapsing into Hanzo's lap.

The archer glanced down to see the man's cheek pressed to his leg. His warm, wet breath brushed Hanzo's skin through his hakama pants and the hairs on the back of his neck bristled, unsure whether he should see the closeness as a threat or a measure of peace.

"Your arrows are silver, huh?" McCree murmured, sounding to be on the edge of sleep. His arms and fingers curled into each other, shrinking his form.

"Sterling. It is sanitary."

"Stings like a bitch."

## My Inside Self

Tram-Anh Tran
FRANKLIN HIGH SCHOOL
WITS WRITER: DAVID CIMINELLO

There are many things that
People think they know about me
This is the me that I have as a façade
On the outside, extremely quiet, timid
Wearing dark-colored hoodies, hiding my arms
Casting off the hint of my interest of anime
Asian facial features, dark black hair
Not a skinny person, but not yet different from others
Extremely tired in school
My outside self is sad and average

There are many things that
People definitely don't know about me
Artistic and imaginative
With gigantic goals for my near future
Wanting to become an animator
People don't know what life is like
I'm physically weak, fearing the seizures
I'm emotionally weak, depressed and scared
Missing my one and only father
My inside self longs for adulthood and justice.

# I See Too Much

Ashwin Thayer
CLEVELAND HIGH SCHOOL
WITS WRITER: COOPER LEE BOMBARDIER

I see it all.

I see my former home rear its shingled head over the horizon. I see the speck of yellow paint that the new coat of lavender could not hide. I see the front yard, with decrepit plants and a flat-tire swing, long since abandoned. I see the driveway. I see a blue Prius, barely covering the space where I once played. I see the door, repainted as if I was supposed to forget. I see a shiny new doorknob with the remnants of a waterlogged tag still attached. I see the hallway. I see shelves filled with spices and jams made from recipes found online. I see the backyard, upkept with a freshly mown lawn. I see the patch of dead grass where our tent stood for years, serving as a fortress for my imagination. I see the stump of the plum tree that I climbed as a child. I see the remains of the shed, wooden planks strewn with flecks of red spotting the wood. I see the flat, empty yard adjacent, where the cornfield was burnt down by a stray cigarette butt from a college student returning home for the holidays.

I see a house, a yard, a driveway.

But I see more than that.

I see my imagination roaming everywhere, grabbing onto anything it can get its hands on. I see the days spent running around and the nights spent sneaking my Game Boy into my room so I could play Pokemon until I fell asleep. I see my mother walking through the front door with a small carrier in her arms, holding a black kitten for my birthday. I see climbing onto the roof when my parents left the house and scraping my hands on the shingles. I see watching cartoons, watching football, watching the first African American President be elected. I see myself grow in the mirror over the days. I see playing Mario Kart in the basement on my Wii. I see my childhood, filled with happiness. I see Thanksgiving dinners and Christmas days and birthdays and I wish I could see it forever, I wish that it was all I saw.

But I see more than that.

I see reality. I see my father passed out on the couch with a needle in his arm. I see him leave, but I don't see him come back. I see the clouds block out the sun during the funeral. I see my mother crying, I see her trying her hardest to raise me alone. I see a man on the other side of the elephant exhibit at the zoo, and I see him talking to my mom. I see their marriage, I see their honeymoon video, I see my new brother, and I see a second bed in a room that was once mine and mine alone. I see my newborn sister and I see her grow up with a learning disability and I see what it means to be born with the odds stacked against you. I see fights, I see myself waking up in the middle of the night to shouting matches upstairs. I see my stepfather sleeping on the couch he was relegated to the previous evening. I see my mother opening the door to my room and telling me that we are moving and I see everything I have lived through flashing through my head until it hurts, until the pain is too much and I can't take it anymore and I have to close my eyes but I still see it all.

I see too much.

## Patterned Thoughts

Connor Henkle
GRESHAM HIGH SCHOOL
WITS WRITER: JAMES GENDRON

A lava spews mountains
a boy speaks truth
Hands mold pyramids and
water guzzles itself

Who are those
who dare to dream?
Like a shooting star shines light
fire glimmers in the night

Journeys through desert plains
masks the feat of man
Let the magma flow
letting go of the patterned thoughts

## Striving for Perfection

Thu Nguyen
FRANKLIN HIGH SCHOOL
WITS WRITER: ALEX BEHR

Jeanette Chen is an extremely smart and outgoing student. According to her friends, she always spends time on the weekend helping out at a homeless shelter. She is known to always have all As in class and is the president of different clubs. But, there is something about her that you might not know—something deep inside that she hides from everybody behind those smiles. Jeanette is never satisfied with herself. Every day, she is living up to her parents' expectations. Jeanette's parents came to the United States from China when she was thirteen years old. They came here to have a new life, with no money and no previous education/knowledge whatsoever. Her family pours all of their immigrants' hopes into her and expects her to do well in school to go to a good college. In addition, her internal pressure is stressing her out to the point that she is never satisfied with herself.

Being the first person to go to college really puts pressure on her. Jeanette's parents are unable to help her with her overall education, for instance, class scheduling and the college application process. In addition, speaking English as a second language is a huge barrier that prevents her from achieving her goals. Jeanette has to put more effort into her work to be as good as her peers. However, she compares herself to them a lot, complaining that even if she puts more effort into her studies, she is never going to be as good as her classmates, who barely study at all.

Anger rises in her body as she receives the test results back from her teacher. It is a B, something she didn't expect after long hours of studying.

"I'm never going to be as good as my classmates," says Jeanette, crumpling the test paper as she speaks. "All of my efforts have gone to waste."

"Listen, why are you beating yourself up over a B when you already have a good grade in this class?" replies Christina, who just got an A.

"It's not about my total grade, it's about my ability. If I don't get a good score on this test, I'm going to do bad on the AP exam."

Recently, her friends have noticed the tired look on her face. Jeanette shows up to school every day with fatigued eyes, hoarse voice, and weary body. Her teachers also notice that she tends to sleep more in class. Jeanette is now suddenly doing poorly in school, just to prepare for her AP exam. Everyday, she goes home and studies until 1:00 or 2:00 in the morning, neglecting the fact that she has to eat to survive. Jeanette functions on a daily basis with four hours of sleep and little eating. Her test results have gotten better, but are those worth the effort of killing herself every day?

As the AP exam approaches, Jeanette finds herself in a hectic state of her life. Not being able to manage her time well due to stress, her schoolwork starts to pile up. She skips school frequently just to stay home and think about how miserable her life is. Jeanette couldn't find her motivation to study for her exam; all she wants to do is to sleep, forever. Christina has tried to confront her about these issues at school, but gets ignored every time. She then talks about Jeanette's problems with the school psychologist to find out what exactly happened.

"I think she is striving for perfection and beating herself up over the fact that she is not as perfect as her peers." The psychologist slips on her tea as she speaks. "This can be a detrimental situation; having someone there for her is super important."

Christina quickly searches for her phone and dials Jeanette's number. The voice from the other side alarms her that something is happening. "What do you want? I don't need you right now. I just want to be alone."

Despite the heavy snowstorm, Christina puts on her heavy jacket and runs to her friend's house as fast as she can. Snow falls more heavily as she sprints through each block. Her legs are trembling from the cold and she can barely feel her hands. As she gets closer to Jeanette's house, she spots a skinny figure standing in the snow, looking up at the starry sky. Christina quickly approaches that person, and embraces the figure.

"I told you not to come, why did you come?" Tears are rolling down Jeanette's cheeks as she starts to kneel down to the ground.

"You are literally the most perfect person I've ever met. So please, don't beat yourself up over how you do in school. It's OK to not be the most perfect person in the world, and it's OK to love yourself and respect how smart and hardworking you are as a person. You tried your best in school, and we all understand that."

Snow stops falling as they speak, as Jeanette looks at the night sky full of blazing stars, finding her true self among those.

# My First Photo

Connor Carr
CLEVELAND HIGH SCHOOL
WITS WRITER: COOPER LEE BOMBARDIER

One of the first photos of me (out of the hundreds my family crammed in our house) is my dad holding me while I'm resting lightly on his forearm. His long and shaggy ponytail rested at the bottom of his back, smoother in contrast to his scratchy beard. I could tell by the look on his face that he loved me. The look I'm not shy to. The crooked smile that radiated love, affection, and endearment. He gazed at my green eyes popping out from the dragonfly nursery clothing given to me by my grandmother. His eyes locked to mine and never left. The way he was holding me with so much fear and support, which only grew stronger as I did. Everything we needed was between us. He knew I was his last, but there was no discontentment in his face. There was no need for anything other than what was right in that moment. There was no hesitation in his love. I could tell that no matter how tall, old, or strong I got, he would always love me unconditionally.

I would always be his baby.

## Colorado Car Troubles

John Lynch
ROOSEVELT HIGH SCHOOL
WITS WRITER: MATTHEW ROBINSON

So we have three friends (Matt, Casey, and Darrell) who are on their way to a NHRA event in Denver when their car breaks down, and they can't figure out what's wrong, they have no cell service, and the closest town is 75 miles away in both directions. So they try to come up with an idea to get out of there.

They have three different ideas: Matt wants to try walking around until he finds cell service, Casey wants to try and just fix the car himself, and Darrell just wants to wait in the car until someone drives by so he can flag them down and ask them for a ride, or for a tow. In the end they have decided to try Casey's idea first, then Darrell's idea, then if all else fails they will try Matt's idea to get the car fixed.

Casey was getting frustrated because no matter how hard he tried to fix the car he just couldn't get it fixed. Darrell was starting to get nervous because what was a normally busy road was starting to seem deserted. While Matt was starting to become upset that Casey and Darrell won't give his idea a try.

Finally Matt snapped and said, "If you two aren't willing to try my idea then I'm going out to try and find the cell service myself."

Casey said, "Matt, the reason we won't try your idea is because it's below freezing outside and we don't have any thick coats to keep warm with. And the fact that we are stranded in the mountains means that we won't find any cell service around here."

Matt countered with, "Well then maybe we could walk around and try to find a cabin, and ask if we can stay there for the night until daylight when it gets a little warmer."

Darrell said, "Even if we could find a cabin around here, it would probably be deserted with just a fireplace, but with no firewood, so we would have to find wood and create a fire ourselves."

Matt finally said, "It's probably better than sleeping in the car all night."

So they continued to argue back and forth, until Casey and Darrell finally relented and said, "Alright Matt we'll go out and look around to try and find a cabin to stay in until the morning."

So they walked around the forest, close to the car, in the freezing cold temperatures and for about half an hour, until they found a cabin. But it was unfortunately abandoned and with no firewood like Darrell thought it would be.

Matt said, "Start grabbing tree branches until we have enough, then we can try to use the wood to start a fire in the fireplace."

So they did and when they had enough to (hopefully) start a small fire they went inside the cabin. Once in the cabin they went to the fireplace, but when they tried to get the fire to light it wouldn't light. And that's when they realized that their wood was too wet, so the fire wouldn't start.

So that's when Darrell said, "We need to try grabbing the lower down limbs, that are more covered if we want to get wood that isn't going to be too wet, but still create a fire."

So they tried again, only this time doing what Darrell said to do to try to get some dry wood. Then they had enough wood to make a fire (hopefully) as long as it was dry enough. So they try again and thankfully it worked, because they were freezing, and they were able to start a fire and warm themselves up a little bit. They were happy that they wouldn't freeze to death, but that quickly faded when two new worries crept up on them.

One was where would they sleep that night, and the other was how were they going to find their car in the morning. To solve the problem of where they would sleep they chose to make beds out of things they could find laying around the cabin and their jackets. So they made beds out of pine needles and sticks then used their jackets to cover up and went to sleep.

When they woke up the fire was out but luckily the storm outside had passed, so they could try and find their way back to the car. When they left the cabin the sun was out but it was still cold outside. So they trudged through the snow until they found their car, and luckily found someone who could give them a tow to the next town. While in the tow truck, Matt, Casey, and Darrell said, "The next time we want to go to an NHRA event in Denver we are flying not driving."

# Metaphor Life

Mayra Mora
GRESHAM HIGH SCHOOL
WITS WRITER: COURTENAY HAMEISTER

My life is like a naked cat. Not many people like or enjoy them but you always find that one person who just loves them to death.

That's basically my high school experience, something bizarre like someone with a foot fetish. Me being the unicorn in the group of asses, I was pretty known, not popular but very well known. I got along with everyone like a burger and fries and I think that's how I met her.

She was a quiet, shy person, nothing like "my type." Then again my type was like a mash of PlayDoh in a daycare. She was the mix of pink and blue that just called my attention. I only had one class with her, science, which was like pulling the winning lottery ticket out of the trash. We didn't sit together, but dang did I try getting her attention—it was like waving traffic signs at a car six feet away from you. My teacher decided to shake up the seating chart and everyone got placed somewhere til there was only four people left, and all I heard was, "Mayra, you're sitting next to Kaitlin." She didn't seem too happy about that. In fact, she looked as if she was thrown a party but didn't get what she wanted.

Kaitlin wasn't very talkative, so I knew that it was my time to shine, and just before my winning pickup line, my teacher told me to shut up. I waited forever for her to have the same feelings. She took her time, too. It was like watching paint dry on all of the Great Wall of China. I was stuck to her like a puppy dog, and eventually she became a dog person. Surprisingly she gave me a shot, but it didn't work out 'cause she was afraid to be hurt, so I made myself into a walking first aid kit.

We began to talk a lot, and we would stay up chatting about things such as whether we would rather fight a robot or badger, and the most random thoughts about if Mike Wazowski blinks or winks, and just like a heater, she warmed up to me and gave me another shot.

Fast forward three exgirlfriends and a cat later, we're going on a year and two months, and soon to be moving into an apartment. I'm no longer the naked cat I once was because what I feel for her is more like puppy love.

## The Noise of Neon

Austin Grantham
LINCOLN HIGH SCHOOL
WITS WRITER: AMY MINATO

The noise of Neon
forcibly removing the only form
pleasure takes, binding me
to what we call life.

Outliving my myth
living longer than life.
I'm not dead,
I'm not living,
I'm only observing.

To cacophonously call upon the oracle
is to call upon myself,
fantasizing that I will never
have a thought again.

I never succeeded or progressed,
stuck in place is where I am.
Gone, glowing,
moving,
laying,
fading.

The will had been written
so I may go,
my life stood tipping over
destined to fall

In my time of demise
the noise of neon shall rise.

# I am an Ear

Emily Carlson
CLEVELAND HIGH SCHOOL
WITS WRITER: COOPER LEE BOMBARDIER

I am an ear.
I see only half of what's going on, but I hear everything.
I hear the scoffs he makes under his breath.
I hear the passive aggressive sighs she makes when she doesn't get her way.
I hear the blood pumping from his heart and through his veins.
I hear the energy he uses to open and close his eyes.
I hear his hungry teeth grinding against themselves.
I hear the sound his palms make when they hold each other and I can hear the air rushing to his lungs with every breath he takes.

*I hear what people don't want me to.*

I hear his stomach growl when he skips lunch and the voice inside his head telling him it's worth it.
I hear his arms giving out as he adds another set to his strenuous workout and I hear the sobs he cries when he can't keep himself from binging on the sweet treats he's hidden in his closet.
I hear the lies he tells himself when he's all alone and the screaming anger in his eyes when he looks in the mirror, still displeased with his body.
I hear his fist meet the mirror, and his eyes meet their reflection in the shattered glass.
I hear him curse to himself under his breath and the tears rolling down his cheek.
I finally hear his heavy, wet eyes coming to a close as he lays his hungry body to rest.
I am his ear.
*I hear everything.*

## two-thousand

Simone Glasgow
FRANKLIN HIGH SCHOOL
WITS WRITER: DAVID CIMINELLO

I know
the hiccup did not go unnoticed
and I know you sighed gently
before you unfurled
on the hardwood floor

and before I carried you to bed
I know
how hard you scrubbed
and I know I heard
a quiet splash
before you went under the bathwater

and before I carried you to bed

I know
I heard you chatter
with the cat
before you pulled her tail
and I know
you yelped before she even
bit you

and before I carried you to bed

## One Day in My Life

Akash Sharma
ROOSEVELT HIGH SCHOOL
WITS WRITER: MATTHEW ROBINSON

My name is Akecheta and I will do anything to protect my family and friends. When I was little my village was set on fire and my grandfather was stuck and couldn't get out. My father and his army tried to save him but it was too late. My life changed ever since. When my grandfather was alive I was always a troublemaker. But whenever I got in trouble my grandfather always got me out and people would get mad at him because he would get me out. But ever since that day I've changed. My dad was chief because my grandfather told everyone and that if something ever happens to him he wants my dad to be chief.

But my life changed because there's this girl that I like. But whenever she talks to me I always make it weird and she walks away like I'm a stranger but truly I just fluke it and I turn red and make things worse. Once she told me that I'm worthless and I'm always trying to impress her but it turns out I'm kinda crazy. My best friend, his name is Etu, he told me that in love, when you want something, let it go or take it. I trust him because we've known each other for about twelve years.

All my life I wanted to catch the biggest salmon for my villages. But my father told me that it takes a lot of courage and I think that I have courage but I can't even talk to a girl. Etu and me go practice to catch fishes but Etu takes no interest in these types of stuff. Whenever I go to the water, Hurit is there (a.k.a. the girl that I like). She has such a good singing voice. Every time we go she's sitting on the rocks and singing and picking shells to make dresses. Seeing her walking picking shells and singing. She just looks beautiful but I just can't tell her.

To get the fish I must make a sharp spear and a few bows then after that we must wait for the time when the biggest salmon comes. Then I have to jump into the water and shoot the arrow but I have to tie the arrow to a rope and throw it to the rocks for it to be stable. Then I must throw the spear and give the signal and have them pull but the hardest part is getting myself to get myself back into the land because the water falls down into a stream. So basically my life's in danger. But anything to keep my loved ones happy.

My father tells me not to do it. But I want to prove I just don't want to be the chef's son. I want to be better than that. But on the other hand my mother and Hurit are scared. But I keep wondering, why does Hurit care if I do it? So later that day I went up to her and I finally had a normal conversation with her then I asked her, "Hurit, why do you care about me?"

She said, "I like you a lot and you're always on my mind and you kinda make me go crazy but why should you care?"

I couldn't reply because it was time to catch the biggest fish. So I kissed her and walked away.

It was time I hugged my mother and told everyone goodbye. But Hurit was crying so I went over there and gave her a big hug and told her, "When I come back I will make you the happiest person here."

My father and other men took me to the water and waited. By then I got all of my stuff ready and waiting. I just needed my father to tell me when to go. He took a moment and closed his eyes and slowly then counted down 5...4...3...2...1 then *splash!*

Everybody looked in and saw me underwater and saw the salmon into its dark black eyes with his wet gills. I shot my bows and hit him into the side and hit him in the head. Then I threw the ropes and got it into the rocks and got it stuck then I swam towards it and flashed the spear into the salmon.

They got the salmon but I was trying to swim back but the water was to strong and it kept pushing me back. They tried to pull on the rope but the water made it snap; people tried to help but couldn't. I held on very tightly and only thing I could remember was was Hurit. I could hear her voice and see her images in my head. I was holding onto a rock and pulled myself up and the people helped me up and I was safe.

They took me back to the village but put me into the back. People thought I was gone but everyone was anxious to know where I was. I popped up from the back and Hurit ran up to me and gave me a big hug.

I was told I was gonna get the biggest piece of fish but I said no because, "We all did this and everyone gets equal amount of fish." People clapped and that night Hurit and I told everything about how we felt about each other.

Hurit asked me one thing, "How did you do it?"

I said, "I thought about you."

## Darkness

Dakota Haddad
GRESHAM HIGH SCHOOL
WITS WRITER: JAMES GENDRON

When you wake up in the morning all you see is darkness. Darkness and emptiness is how you can see my future. Like my parents always tell me I should be ashamed and should not try and touch the stars because I'm nothing. I am like the noises you hear at night, annoying and unloveable. I am like the part in the salad you do not eat.

## 911

Jacob Bolger
CLEVELAND HIGH SCHOOL
WITS WRITER: COOPER LEE BOMBARDIER

The kitchen of my house where I grew up was very small. The whole family would always want to be in that one room; people would be trying to walk to the one small doorway into the living room. We have a large table in our kitchen and behind it there was stairs that go into our basement.

One specific memory I have about my kitchen is when my dad was putting in new steps that lead to our basement. He was strong but I didn't think he was strong enough to do it himself.

I saw little individual drops of sweat dripping down the side of his face so I asked him, "Do you want the big strong police to come and help you?"

"No no, Jacob, don't call the police."

So I ran to find my mom who was working on dinner. I said, "Mommy where is the 1 on the phone?"

She pointed to it so I pressed down on the nine. I ran into my room and pressed down on the one twice to complete the phone number and I pressed *call*. My mom came bursting into my room and grounded me immediately.

I'll never forget how to dial 911.

## Everything Was Fine

Makayla Barton
BENSON HIGH SCHOOL
WITS WRITER: KATHLEEN LANE

Everything was fine until it wasn't.

I roll over and look at my phone with tired eyes to see I have a text from my sister. It reads, "I'm fine, pray for my friends."

You know the sinking feeling you get in your stomach when you're going to a new place, your phone's dead and you realize you're completely lost and have no idea where you are? That doesn't even begin to describe the way I'm feeling right now.

I tell her not to leave, I tell her to stay in state, stay near what's familiar, stay near me. I can't go to her, she is so far from me, so close to the danger.

I pull myself out of bed and turn on the TV. The weather is on. It's going to be 73 degrees today. The lady has a nice green dress on. She's cracking jokes. Does she not know about the horror that could be going on? I don't have to look hard to find it; school shootings always make top news.

I can't quite comprehend the words coming out of the reporter's mouth: "Thirteen dead, killer still actively shooting." My mind is racing. Time is moving so slow, I don't think there is a word to describe the absolute terror I am feeling right now.

I'm not sure if minutes or hours have passed but somehow I'm now on the floor.

There's a man on TV who appears to be waiting to be interviewed, possibly going to share how he was connected to the victims. He's going to share about how the last two or three years were such an honor.

Behind the professor is chaos. I can count six ambulances and what seems to be millions of cop cars. There are people just waiting to break through the caution tape and go hold their loved loves, some are in heaps on the ground after hearing more terrible news.

The man is wearing a grey suit with a navy blue bow tie. The kind I want at my wedding. Then I see it, his pretty pale skin has wine red tracing unforgettable lines across his face, dipping down into the dimple on his left cheek. His hands in tight cuffs making it impossible for him to fire another shot at innocent victims. His smile is plastered on, just like in the movies.

## Dear Hands

Jared Alton
ROOSEVELT HIGH SCHOOL
WITS WRITER: JOANNA ROSE

You have always been by my side, whether you wanted to or not. There are so many lines across your palms—are they called palms because the lines are like the roots of a palm tree, or are the lines scars of a past life that I did not share with you? Do you try to hold me back? Sorry for the pun but you should know I'm not done—this is just too much fun. If you dislike it you could stop—you're the one writing. I merely suggest what to write. You consider if it's right, of course. You're not stopping. I knew it. You love it! Oh my sweet hands, how you do everything for me! You let me play games, you cook for me, and, oddly, I have never heard you complain.

## Recollection

Natalie Perkins
FRANKLIN HIGH SCHOOL
WITS WRITER: DAVID CIMINELLO

I remember
those marks you left on me
you said
"it won't happen again
I promise"
but did you mean it?

those bottles of whiskey
you left lying around
the dirty little habit
of drinking so much
that you forgot
the holes you left in the walls
and the black eyes
you left on me

"I didn't think
it would hurt you
baby"
you claimed
but I don't believe you anymore
finally
I remember

I remember
finally
but I don't believe you anymore
"baby
it wouldn't hurt you
I didn't think"

you left on me
the black eyes and
the holes you left in the walls
that you forgot
from drinking so much.
the dirty little habit
you left lying around
those bottles of whiskey

but did you mean it?
"I promise
it won't happen again"
you said
those marks you left on me
I remember

# No Apologies

Abby Wolf
LINCOLN HIGH SCHOOL
WITS WRITER: BRIAN KETTLER

*The stage is dark. Center stage there is an amber spotlight on a beautifully set table and a fancy coat hanger. Upstage left there is a dimmer and smaller amber spotlight on a podium where a waitress dressed in five star waiter attire stands. Kent is dressed in formal business attire and holds a briefcase, a manila folder, and a crisp white envelope. Jessabelle wears a short black form-fitting dress, chunky heeled boots, and a black leather trench coat. Her makeup is sultry and dark. She does not look trashy, instead she looks wealthy and in charge. Her femininity and power makes Kent visibly uncomfortable.*

*(lights go up on the podium)*

KENT
*(enter next to podium)* Reservation for Kent?

WAITRESS
*(checks off something in reservation book)* Yes, right this way, sir.
*(lights go up on table. Kent takes off his blazer and hands it to the waitress who hangs it up as he sits down)*

WAITRESS
Anything to drink, sir?

KENT
Yes, bring me your finest scotch, no ice.

*(waitress exits stage right and enters with a crystal glass of scotch and a glass of ice)*

KENT
I said no ice! Ice on the side is still ice.

WAITRESS
My apologies, sir. *(takes ice and exits, enters stage left by podium)*
*(Enter Jessabelle stage left where Kent entered. Jessebelle hangs up her coat.)*

WAITRESS
Hello, do you hav—

JESSABELLE
*(walks by to the table, hushing the waiter by holding her hand up)* Hello, I believe you're who I'm here to speak with.

KENT
Indeed I am, I'm—

JESSABELLE
Stop. No names; I told you this when you contacted me.

KENT
*(awkwardly)* Oh, yes, that's right. May I buy you a drink?

JESSABELLE
An old-fashioned, thanks.

KENT
Waiter!

WAITRESS
*(leaves podium and comes to the table)* Yes, sir?

KENT
An old-fashioned for the lady.
*(waitress exits stage right and re-enters stage right with an old-fashioned and sets it in front of Jessabelle without a word)*

JESSABELLE
Thank you, ma'am. *(hands the waitress a few dollars)*

KENT
That's quite a drink for a pretty little lady like you to be ordering.

JESSABELLE
*(calmly)* I didn't come here to flirt with you, I came here to talk about doing something for you that you're too cowardly to do yourself. If all you want is a skanky whore to buy drinks for and flirt with you've come to the wrong place. *(mutters to herself)* This is why I don't work for men. *(stands up and reaches for her coat)*

KENT
No! Wait, I'm sorry.

JESSABELLE
Good, you should be. *(sits back down and sips on her drink)* Fuck that's a good old-fashioned. *(drinks a little more)* Also, here's a hint for the future; next time you meet with a woman who could make you disappear without a trace, don't piss her off. I don't work for men; they all try and pull this shit.

KENT
I'm terribly sorry.

JESSABELLE
So what can I do for you? *(Kent slides manila folder over and she opens it)*

JESSABELLE
Shit.

KENT
Is there a problem?

JESSABELLE
Yes. I used to know him. I can't do this. I can't hit people that I have ties to. The Feds could find me.

KENT
I don't care. I need him dead.

JESSABELLE
I won't do it.

KENT
I'll pay you $500,000. If I'm correct that's over twice what you charge.

JESSABELLE
You'd be paying me to go to the chair. Someone else would happily do it for that much but that person isn't me.

KENT
Well, I suppose my money doesn't talk. I didn't want to do this but you're leaving me no choice. I need him dead. *(slides another envelope to her)*

JESSABELLE
*(opens envelope)* Oh you dirty bastard. *(gets up to leave)*

KENT
*(grabs her wrist)* You think I don't have duplicates of those photos?

JESSABELLE
*(sits back down)* You think this is the first time I've been blackmailed?

KENT
I chose you because you're good at your job. I could send you to the electric chair on these photos alone.

JESSABELLE
*(relaxes and pretends to think)* I'd still get the five hundred?

KENT
That's what I offered isn't it?

JESSABELLE
Fine. I'll do it. Under one condition.

KENT
And what would that be?

JESSABELLE
You pay me now and give me the duplicates.

KENT
Okay. *(hands her the briefcase)* You'll find your payment, a flash drive, and a memory card containing the photos. I want you to do this one differently. Don't seduce him. I want you to go into his apartment at night and shoot him in the back of his head with a silenced pistol.

JESSABELLE
I can do that. Photos will be in the mail when I've finished.

BLACKOUT

JESSABELLE
Oh, and Kent?

KENT
Yes?

*(a gunshot is heard along with Kent's body hitting the floor)*

JESSABELLE
Don't ever blackmail a trained killer.

END

# The Kitchen

Jobana Guzman
CLEVELAND HIGH SCHOOL
WITS WRITER: COOPER LEE BOMBARDIER

Cold floors and the smell of burnt tortillas. Usually bright mornings and dark nights—the clear back door, cold to touch. My mother always by the stove cooking up some new "magical dish" which would either turn out to be amazing or a disaster.

The place she would peek her head out from everyday after school to greet me. The place where Thanksgiving dinners turned into playing loud music and laughing about the most random things. The places where we'd have competitions to see who could eat the most tacos. Where an empty fish bowl sits on the counter after the last death in the family (R.I.P. Pollo). The place where I'd hide in—an empty cupboard when we'd play hide and seek. The place where I'd sneak into at the crack of dawn to grab a snack for my Netflix binging.

The kitchen—the place where the best secrets are spilled. What is said in the kitchen stays in the kitchen.

## Only Through His Eyes

Ramatoulaye Thioub
GRANT HIGH SCHOOL
WITS WRITER: ARTHUR BRADFORD

I sat, pounding my fists into the hard rubber pieces that lay in between the long green plastic strings that are made to look like grass. I could feel the red stigma cover the creases of my face as I sat. Furious. *What's wrong with me? Why can't I just be normal?* I was trying my best but it took every nerve in my body to just say hi. Why is that so hard? I felt like I couldn't speak, though I was desperate to let the flow of air exhale my body. *I want to go home. I'm scared.*

It was a beautiful day. The sun had rose to angle in the beautiful blue sky that made the light seem to have run on forever. I woke up in the happiest mood, excited to see my friends at the park. I got ready quickly making sure to remember my ball, cleats, and backpack. In the backpack, I packed the necessities for a stereotypical teenager: a few snacks, some water, and a phone charger in case it died during the day. I hopped on my bike, whose seat was scorching hot from the sunlight that rested upon its rubber, and was on my way to Grant High School.

It had been months since the bottom of my cleats had brushed through a field of grass, attempting to strike the center of a ball each time. I had chosen baseball over soccer, though it is the sport that almost all my friends still currently play. It was exhilarating being out again, though the droplets of sweat began to bombard the top of my forehead, as the blazing hot sun struck my pale skin, turning it a shade of pink. The occasional breeze ran through the flow of my long blonde hair each time I swayed from side to side.

I finally arrived as I watched Emma wave me over to the last goal that was open. Emma was outgoing and fun and soccer was one of the biggest things we bonded over. We began with shooting. I remember hitting some balls on target though a lot of them were off. After a while, we took a break and then went out for lunch.

On the way back we ran into a group of friends that we had maybe talked to once or twice over the media but never in person for me.

Emma was fearless and incredibly, her encounters with new people were admirable. I wish talking to a group of people could be that easy, but I could already feel my body raging with nerves as she pulled us closer towards them. My gut was telling me not to go, but it was already too late.

"Hi," "hey" "what's up," were only a few of the expressions yelled out of what felt like a billion. I just wanted to run away. It was way too much to handle. I quickly waved and told Emma I'd be back. Panting hard, as my breath increased faster, I jogged over to our bags.

The voice running through the back of my head continued to run through my brain. It makes me second, third, and sometimes fourth-guess my decisions, which sends me into a whole new level of stress. I love my friends and I do love my family, but pushing myself to be around them all at once makes my body anxious. I panic constantly. Always Rush. Live in regret. And push away the people who really care. I just want to have fun without worrying. I want to be able to hang out with everybody, without feeling overwhelmed, but social anxiety has been running over my entire body for years. Nobody understands it, and I don't think it's ready to go away anytime soon.

## One of the Horsemen

Atticus Larsen
ROOSEVELT HIGH SCHOOL
WITS WRITER: JOANNA ROSE

4 horsemen and you're one of them.
You great riddler of diseases and disasters: unbridled faith
sweats out of your swollen glands
making everyone choke and cough.
You bring pestilence,
like your brothers and sisters,
become a junkie; a junkie
of sweet sassafras in the form of antibiotics—
twist and turn and dance and cry
like the bringer of death on the wind.
It carries throughout your small frame
until it reaches the brain. Then starts again
in another host.
You bringer of insomniacs and living nightmares.
You germ-bringing hellion atop a thieving nucleus.
Perhaps you just need some soap
but
that's just a quiet idea in my sick brain.

## A Twisted Mind

Cleda Hodes
BENSON HIGH SCHOOL
WITS WRITER: KATHLEEN LANE

"You ready to get out of here?" Scarlett said, unlocking the barred window and linking her fingers to give me a step up.

"Let's do this," I said, overly confidently. Inside I was terrified. I stepped on her hands, pulling myself up.

We heard another horrifying scream from the room next to us and all I could think about was getting out of this dreaded place. I was out of the window, ready to pull up Scarlett when Ryan came stumbling into the room, giving us an uncomfortable direct stare. He seemed like a confused dog tilting his head, trying to make sense of what was happening. He had always given me the chills in his white straitjacket, his hands trapped. With stuttered words he barely managed to say, "T-ta-ake me wit-th you."

That was the first time I had ever heard Ryan speak. It was a little shocking.

I knew we couldn't take him, but the thought of him stuck in this broken place made my heart sink in my chest. This place was awful. They treated us as if we weren't even human. This place was 100 times worse than prison. It was full of broken people who had given up on life, like zombies of their old selves with the hundreds of medications and tests they forced us into doing.

I gave Ryan an apologetic look. I wanted to help him so badly but Scarlett was more heartless and just said, "Ryan, face it, you will never get out of here, it's a fact."

"You are so heavily watched, we would be stupid to take you," she carried on as she reached up for my hands.

As I pulled her up she locked the window, putting the key in her bra and quickly grabbing my arm.

We ran through the long grass in the yard. We stopped the second we heard a shriek of car tires outside the large gate. We ducked instantaneously. Scarlett was hidden perfectly with her long dark hair covering most of her body, camouflaging her into the dead of night.

It was strange to have anyone come even near this place. We were approximately fifteen miles away from the closest town.

The car flashed its headlights on and off five times, two slow, two fast, and one slow. Scarlett looked at me and whispered, "Follow me."

I followed her not necessarily because I trusted her but because I had nowhere else to go. We army crawled through the grass and crawled under the fence with help from a small hole we buried under the gate prior to this. As we got to the car the man inside never got out. The most I could see of him was that he was a skinny bald white man with a scar on the top left of his head just like Scarlett's. Of course hers was harder to see. Her hair covered most of it.

The trunk of the car opened and Scarlett guided me in, telling me, "Hide here, we will get out at the next town over. It's going to be a long drive."

I got in and I couldn't see much but the red taillights, making it barely possible to see Scarlett's face. Her face seemed so perfect until you saw the scar. She was like a Barbie who got damaged. I saw the trunk close and that was the last time I ever saw or even heard of Scarlett Briggs. To the rest of the world she never existed. I don't remember what happened the rest of that night, only I woke bandaged up a week later in some man's house.

Fifteen years later from the day of the escape, I got a letter from Scarlett stating: "Dear Olivia, I am so glad to see that you have fully recovered. I see that you have been good, well, I mean as good as you can be, I know you know what I mean. Anyways I need you to come back to the asylum on Saturday the 28th. Oh and make sure to bring one weapon of choice. Remember. If you don't you will regret it. Not to mention I can put you back into the asylum in a snap of my fingers. Anyways that's all. Can't wait to see you. It will be a night to remember. XOXO Scarlett."

I dropped the note at my feet. My heart fell deep in my chest and I couldn't move. I was terrified for my life, and what might happen next.

I could barely sleep knowing that in the morning it would be the 28th and I had to go to the asylum. I somehow managed to get dressed and out into my little car. I knew it was going to be a long drive so I needed to get going before Scarlett came after me. I just grabbed a cardigan and left. I was thinking about bringing a weapon, but I knew that if I did there would be no point. I don't have the heart to use a weapon to hurt someone, and I do not want my weapon to be used against anyone, even if I'm not the one using it, so I didn't bring a weapon.

Once I reached the towering black gates of the asylum, awful memories just came flooding in my head, but I knew I couldn't focus on any of that. I noticed there were thirty or so people all huddled around Scarlett. Except for four bodyguards around the perimeter with guns in their hands. I have no idea how Scarlett got her own bodyguards or why she even needed them. I was about to go back into my car and drive away as far as I could get when I heard Scarlett say, "Oliva there you are. You here are the last one we were waiting for." Gesturing to the bodyguards, Scarlett said, "Let her in."

One of the extraordinarily tall bodyguards came over and opened the gate. The second I walked in he locked the gate. I felt an eerie vibe from everything, but I kept walking till I was with everyone else.

Once I was there Scarlett started saying, "So happy to see all of you guys here. Not like you had much of a choice." Scarlett continued talking while pulling a handgun out of the belt of her pants. "So basically I need the most insane one out of all of you. To find out who that may be let's play a little game. The rules are simple. Last person standing wins. If anyone tries to escape you will be killed immediately. If you take too long you will be killed. If anyone even looks like they are going after me they will be killed in a blink of an eye. I hope you all chose the right weapon because your objective is to kill everyone except for me of course...Oh, and yourself. Good luck and remember, have fun." She said *have fun* as if we were playing Jenga or in summer camp.

"Oh I almost forgot," Scarlett said while loading her handgun, "just so you all take this seriously. Bring him out." She looked over at the tall bodyguard who was grabbing some man with a black bag on his head and guiding him in front of Scarlett. When he took off the guy's bag I couldn't believe my eyes. It was Ryan, the guy I could've saved.

Scarlett was holding the handgun one inch from Ryan's face and I sprinted. Before I knew it I was in between Ryan and the gun, acting as a human shield. I closed my eyes as tightly as I could, waiting for my death. It took too long I thought, so I slowly opened my eyes and I could see Scarlett's hand reaching out to me. Scarlett said, "Congratulations, we have a winner. Olivia, by sacrificing your life for his, a guy who you abandoned earlier, shows that you have…"

A sharp gun sounded and Scarlett's lifeless body fell directly on top of me. I rolled her ragdoll of a body off of me, and began to weep. Even though she had a twisted mind and was a terrible human, seeing someone die in person scars you. I hated Scarlett and everything she did. She was about to kill everyone else, yet still I couldn't help it, my tears fell down my face, leaving my face soaked.

Ryan, who I had completely forgotten about, wrapped his arms around me and just held me as I broke down in his arms.

With the death of Scarlett Briggs also came the death of my living nightmare. I was finally, truly free from Scarlett and her twisted mind.

# I Remember

Monica Nesta Beltran
FRANKLIN HIGH SCHOOL
WITS WRITER: DAVID CIMINELLO

I remember when life used to be colorful.
Before age 9 life was simple
All I remember doing was enjoying being a kid
I remember being 6 and breaking a bone
I tried avoiding going to the hospital
But I had no choice
I remember being 7 and enjoying our vacations in Mexico
Summer nights consisted of diving
Under the bed sheets
The reason?
Thunder
I remember when life used to be colorful...
Before age 9 life was simple
After age 9, life's color slowly started to fade away
I remember being 10 and
Worrying about my weight
I remember being 11 and having different methods
To lose weight
I remember being 12 and being hungry
I remember during that summer in Mexico
I wouldn't swallow my food
I kept my mouth glued
I remember being 13 and having family calling me
Pretty and asking me how I lost weight
I remember 13-year-old Monica being proud of herself
She lied about eating when she was offered food
She lied that the way of losing weight was eating correctly and exercising
And everyone believed her
I remember 13-year-old Monica
Asking herself why they called her pretty

Now that she was skinnier
And not before that
I guess "It's not what's on the outside that matters, it's what's on the inside"
Was just BS
I remember being 14 and laughing all day
But crying when I was alone
I remember being 14 and having friends
Yet I felt alone
I remember blaming myself for everything
Saying sorry even when it wasn't my fault
But I thought it was
I remember having thoughts...
Thoughts that could get me in trouble
My thoughts weren't hurting anyone,
Except one person
Myself
I remember secretly asking adults for help
It didn't work at all because all I got in return was either
"It's all in your head, you're fine"
Or
"You're just going through a phase"
"You're fine"
And I guess they were right
"I'm fine, just tired"
Tired of being my own enemy
Tired of looking in the mirror
Tired of hating my reflection
Tired of trying
The list can keep going but I guess I'll stop here
Cause I'm tired

I remember when life used to be colorful
Before age 9
Now life seems to have lost all its colors
The colors that were once bright
Are now drained
Making life seem grey

## Conscious

Kai Field
LINCOLN HIGH SCHOOL
WITS WRITER: AMY MINATO

Jellyfish bobbed around the glass cage, giving no thought to the fact that this was not their native environment. Rather, it was an aquarium tank inside a restaurant. Leo patiently sat at booth twenty-eight with his family, waiting for his steak. Suddenly the urge hit him—the need to find a restroom. Leo looked to his father, excused himself, and bounded to the men's room.

On his way back, he noticed the tank: a seven-foot-tall glass rectangle extending from a three-foot block on the floor to the ceiling, filled to the brim with jellyfish, all gracefully moving about their space. Leo was mesmerized; he had never seen a jellyfish before. He glanced around the restaurant, spotted a waiter, and waved his hand. The server approached.

"Excuse me, sir, what are these creatures behind the glass?" Leo wondered aloud.

"Young man, you mean to tell me you've never seen a jellyfish before?" The waiter responded, shocked.

"A jellyfish? No. Never."

"Well, child of table twenty-eight, a jellyfish is a fine species of the Cnidaria phylum."

Leo had no idea what a phylum was or what it meant to be part of the Cnidaria phylum, so he pretended to understand and lost himself in the bioluminescent animals freely roaming the cage.

The waiter continued to fire facts about the jellyfish, until he realized that Leo was no longer paying attention. He ignored the rudeness and said, "Beautiful, aren't they?"

"Definitely." Leo turned back to the waiter and asked, "Where did you find them?"

"Oh, we hire special jellyfish catchers to go down to Alben Beach to find them."

"That's cool," Leo said, admiring the jellyfish and their bobbing behavior.

A bell rang from the kitchen, "Well, young man, that's my call, I'm glad you like the jellyfish."

The waiter ran back to the kitchen to retrieve and deliver his next order.

Leo stared into the tank of glowing marine animals and sighed. He'd fallen in love with these delicate beings. Then he realized that his family must be waiting for him. He rushed back to his table just as a waitress set down his steak, medium well, just as he liked it.

Leo began to eat his steak, glancing back to the jellyfish as he ate. He stared at the jellyfish for a while, unconsciously blocking out his parents' worried questions. After five more questions and some panicked pokes to the back, his parents finally gave up their "kind act" and poured a glass of water on his head. Leo finally snapped out of his delicate jellyfish examination and turned around, glaring at them like an irritated devil cat.

"Leo, now that we've got your attention, you've been in a trance for the past ten minutes and you're beginning to eat the fork."

Leo took the fork out of his mouth and was shocked to see he had bent all four tines.

"Alright, Lion, let's just go home." His father shook his head. "I'll set down a generous tip for them to buy a new fork," he added forgivingly.

Leo stood up, grabbed his mother's hand, and looked at the jellyfish one more time as he and his family started for the door. His eyes widened as all the jellyfish stopped to watch him go, a few even waved their tentacles as he walked out the door. Leo couldn't help but wave back.

On the drive home, they passed the ocean. Leo leaned against the car door and watched the sea glisten, he felt like it was calling to him. He scrunched his eyes, and looking closer, he saw floating lights, all as vibrant as the previous jellyfish. He thought he was hallucinating, but every time he looked away and back, they were still there. Leo watched them until he fell asleep.

When he awoke, his father was pulling into the driveway. Leo got out of the car, went upstairs to his room, and sat at his desk. He flicked his desk lamp on and off a couple times, then took out a pen and piece of paper. He looked back into his memory on how the probable hallucinations of jellyfish over the sea looked, and doodled them all over his paper. Then he took out his markers, various neon shades, and started to color the jellyfish. However, he challenged himself to go beyond the lines, because that's how the jellyfish looked—splatters of color everywhere. He examined his drawing carefully and, satisfied, put his supplies away and taped it to the wall in front of his bed. Then he gathered his clothes, and went to the bathroom to take a shower.

He turned on the water and went in. He stood there blankly, under the artificial waterfall. He closed his eyes and sighed. When he opened them, he saw neon lights pouring out of the showerhead, but he did not grow anxious. He simply stood as the colors enclosed around him, wrapping him in a rainbow cocoon. It was as if he were a corpse, and the neon illuminations were trying to give him back his life. Leo closed his eyes and held his head back as the water pounded against his chest like a gorilla to its own. He could feel jolts of energy swarming through his body. And then it stopped. His mother was calling. Leo opened his eyes and watched the lightshow retreat back into the showerhead, lost in the transparent sea.

"Yeah?" he called back to his mother, lowering the water pressure to hear her better.

"Are you taking a shower?!"

"Yes!"

"Okay! Just making sure!"

Leo turned the water back on and stared at the wall, trying to make sense of what he'd just experienced. A few minutes later, he squatted down on the floor and wrapped his arms around his legs. He watched the shower droplets stream down his legs like small rivers, making their way into the drain. Leo smiled as he sat, picturing himself standing on the beach, toes in the sand. The sun warming his skin. Leo could see the horizon, where the ocean and sky met. He could almost smell the seaweed-scented environment, taste the salty water, hear the gulls calling from the rocks. He had always loved the ocean, since the first grade, when he learned about its infinite mass and its large population of aquatic wildlife. Leo beamed with joy, he couldn't possibly be burdened with waiting a moment longer. He had to see the jellyfish again.

He got out of the shower, got dressed, and sprinted back into his room. He grabbed a sticky note and wrote *I went to the beach to see the jellyfish again*. With that, he threw on his shoes, raced down the stairs, and out the door. He ran down the highway, along cars, leading to

Alben Beach. After forty minutes of running, the ten-year-old finally made it. He stopped at the rocks just below the highway, looked up at the dark clouds, closed his eyes, and smiled. Once again, glowing lights lit up the surface of the water in the overcast night. Leo watched them like a deer in the shadows, making sure it was safe.

One of the lights sprang from the low tide and floated towards him, stopping inches away from his face. It hovered there until one of its tentacles grabbed his arm. It tugged him, signaling for him to come into the water with the rest of them. Leo blinked and followed the little jellyfish into the soft currents of the ocean, which were also pulling him into the open ocean. Once the water reached his chest, Leo fainted and the jellyfish swarmed his body, creating a surrounding glow.

His body began to look transparent and his beating heart was in view. His skin turned jellylike and his clothes disappeared. He started to shrink, and become rounder. Leo was turning into a jellyfish. Then, fully transformed, Leo was a jellyfish that flashed all the colors of the rainbow, the most beautiful of them all.

Leo's parents had driven down to the beach and stood at the foot of the tides, worried about the whereabouts of their missing son. Leo noticed his parents jump out of the car and run down to the sand. He then took his human form again and walked atop the water to his parents, who stood there confused and worried. Leo stopped in front of them, transparent and flashing rainbow colors, he held out his hands and smiled. His parents each grabbed one of them, Leo squeezed their hands and let go, an unspoken way of saying *I love you and I'll miss you*.

He transformed back into a jellyfish, waved a tentacle, and floated back into the ocean where thousands of other jellyfish met him. His parents watched as Leo met his fate and began his new life with the jellyfish, all disappearing into the night. Leo's mother hugged her husband and started crying, but she knew this event would mark the beginning of a newfound joy that Leo would experience. Now Leo could be king, a lion among jellyfish.

## Aftermath

Manoj Bhukar
BENSON HIGH SCHOOL
WITS WRITER: KATHLEEN LANE

The day that my mother wished me goodnight was like every night at home. But when I woke up in the wee hours of the morning, I was in bed with clothes scattered, as if a tornado had hit. I called down the silent house. I looked up to see millions of stars everywhere except for one. That's when I knew that someone had been taken away. The coldness of the morning sank into my skin. I slipped out of my bed and walked into a different world.

The sweat from the hot morning dampened my socks. I walked onwards in this unreal place. The odor of raw sewage hit my face and the intensity of it made me walk faster. Now and then I could see black birds swooping down and eating grains from the rice fields, recently harvested. The sound that pushed me onwards was the chattering and weeping of people. I walked onwards as though in a daze. I looked left and right, looking for why they were all despondent and then saw. I saw it.

The face of a woman, her brown eyes frozen, looking up. A jagged knife wound ran down her whole chest, which was covered in a sea of blood. I looked around. The tears of people spilled like raindrops. Their grief struck me later when I walked alone searching for my mother. I waited and waited. I slept and waited for days, but she never came.

I began to dry up of tears. I sat frozen in time like playdough that had been left out to dry.

# Rainbow Colored Sticky Notes

Ana Shepherd
GRANT HIGH SCHOOL
WITS WRITER: ARTHUR BRADFORD

Her backpack weighed nearly fifteen pounds. It was a bright periwinkle blue, so new you could smell it. On the front of it a wide assortment of pins and patches were stuck, carrying various slogans such as, "I'm still with her" or "pro choice."

At the very bottom of her bag lay a crisply folded suit jacket, black and stiff. Neatly stacked upon her jacket lay exactly three books, varying in size: *Freedom For Women* by Carol Giardina, *The Boundaries of Her Body* by Debran Rowland, and *Man's Dominion* by Sheila Jeffreys. Pages upon pages of these books were dog eared and marked with an array of rainbow colored sticky notes, which contained quotes and statistics, written in dark, neat lettering. If you were to open one of these three novels, you'd find that the margins had been written in: stickers were posted over facts, opinions boasted in all caps either agreeing or not.

His bag, however, was rather different. It was black and horribly battered. Inside, a large selection of candy wrappers from years ago lay scattered at the bottom. Thrown upon these carelessly discarded wrappers lay exactly three rather thin magazines. Their covers ranged from very nearly naked women to others who were very much unclothed and stretched across many-colored sporting vehicles in a seemingly uncomfortable manner. Stuffed hastily underneath the provocative images were two small containers of unscented lotion. In the small zipper pocket at the side of his beat-up bag, was a red toothbrush.

Its bristles contained bits of dried Crest toothpaste and its ends were worn and splitting. Wadded up was an old $100 bill. This bit of dirty currency, he believed, would be sufficient enough to get him far, far away.

## Nervous, Anxious, Relieved

Isabella Nguyen
ROOSEVELT HIGH SCHOOL
WITS WRITER: MATTHEW ROBINSON

Kae'lyn Ann Tinio, a female who has long dark brown hair, hazel brown eyes, flawless baby smooth skin, a nice petite body, average height, voice high pitched but not as high, a cheerleader, dancer, and track runner, and a Honor Roll sophomore in high school in Los Angeles, California. She's such a positive student who knows her right and wrongs. Worries well about large social issues. Loves helping people and is a big student in the school. Always fun to be around but knows when to be serious at times.

But today, April 20th, it's Thursday and she has never performed in front of the whole school during a assembly before. It's making her nervous from doing all of her school work. The assembly is going to be filled with students, staff, her friends, those who don't like her, and many others.

As the day continues it's eighth period and she has to go meet up with her team to get ready, thinking about it more and more, worrying about how close time is, she gets nervous and nervous each time.

The whole team is playing music, trying to forget about the time and that they have to perform soon, all happy and singing at the top of their lungs to good music.

It's time now. They rush downstairs out of the dance studio to the gym, sitting together on the bleachers waiting until it's time for them to perform, after the announcements and the other events that are going on in the assembly.

Now they are up. Her heart is beating faster than ever, already sweating from being nervous, and her hands start shaking. They walk onstage while being announced to the crowd. They straighten their line as they get ready to start their dance.

The dance is a story about racism, white privilege, and is full of strong emotions. They also performed this for their state competition. They do their stomp-in to get to their spot on the floor, then the music starts. As she dances throughout the full routine, she loses her fear, her nervousness, and becomes very confident and comfortable.

They finish their dance and exit off the floor; they cheer around together as a team, proud and excited because they overcame their fear of dancing in front of the school with a powerful message.

They go back inside the gym to cheer other events and performances. After all the performances, their coach comes up to them and congratulates them on the way they performed and then after the team left the gym to find a quiet space to continue talking, everyone was very happy and was shocked to see such a powerful dance like that. After the coach finished talking, they did their all hands in and yelled, "Velts Up!" and clapped three times—a routine every time they finish a team talk.

After everything they had to do, they decided to all go take team pictures by the photo booth. They took serious, silly, random, and many more different types of pictures. People started to leave the gym, and so then Kae'lyn's mom arrived to pick her up.

She left. In her mind she was relieved after everything; she was very happy that she overcame her fear of dancing in front of the school just from dancing and zoning herself out from the crowd and focusing on the dance and feeling it as if no one was around.

After thinking about the performance, she goes on and starts talking to her mom about how everything went, talking all excited and happy.

## Only in Portland

Jezebel Herrera
FRANKLIN HIGH SCHOOL
WITS WRITER: DAVID CIMINELLO

Only in Portland you can hear gunshots
Going "Bang! Bang!"
From the back of my house.
Only in Portland you can witness most men threatening their wives, girlfriends,
just because
They didn't listen, even sometimes you witness them beating on their girls.
Only in Portland you can hear, see people screaming and yelling at each other.
Only in Portland you see high-speed chases as the police speed down your street to catch up to the person
Only in Portland you can see sketchy people
Swapping drugs for money.
Only in Portland you can witness someone pull a knife or gun on someone
Only in Portland you see families happy and cheerful walking to and from the park.

## Outdoor School

Mitchell Rose
CLEVELAND HIGH SCHOOL
WITS WRITER: ALEX BEHR

Sellwood looked different in the morning. After two months, the faded white walls with the dark green edges were easily recognized. But when the lingering sun cast pale shadows on the canvas of my school, something new was created.

Our dented car kicked loose gravel from the pavement as it heaved itself into the staff parking lot. We were still ten minutes early, but I could see others had already arrived. Even if I didn't know who they were, I could always recognize other sixth graders. Remembering passing them in the hall, from trying to inch my way past them, hugging the lockers, as they stood in the middle of the hall, loudly talking to friends. But even if I hadn't seen them before, it wasn't hard to tell they were sixth graders: how tall they were, how they walked, the clothes they wore. Every detail was calculated in my head before I gave a verdict. A couple of them were spotted immediately, carrying overstuffed backpacks, or duffle bags with clothes hanging out. They looked like they were prepared for weeks, hiking through isolated Canadian forests, or scaling treacherous, corpse-riddled, mountain trails. Way too much for a three-day trip. Admittedly, I was over prepared myself, carrying a gym bag with an extra pair of everything I was told to bring. We pulled into the vice-principal's spot.

"Here we are," Dad said. "You got everything ready?"

I finished surveying my surroundings, and turned to the driver's seat to respond. "Yeah," I said, tightening my grip on the rough strap of the bag.

"Alright well, I guess I'll see you on Saturday."

"Yeah, I'll see ya too."

If my life was a book, sixth grade would be a chapter you could skip. It wasn't a particularly bad time in my life, but it certainly wasn't good. It was a chapter with a lot of description and not much action—where the words get repetitive and lose meaning as you just stare, uncomprehendingly at the page while your mind turns to something else to think about. Not that nothing interesting happened in that year; there was plenty that happened. It's easy to look at your past self with distaste, a younger more naïve version of myself is just so easy to ridicule. It's easy because I know everything about him, and there's nothing he can do to fight back. Coincidentally, 6th grade was also the year I grew aware of possible criticisms from the future (although I took revenge by insulting my eighth-grade self, in a required letter to the future). I believed my seemingly inconsequential, coin-flip choices would usher in an impending dystopian version of my life.

Entering through the front doors, I faced a surprisingly empty hallway. The unusual school of the morning also had an unusual interior. The fluorescent lights that still worked illuminated pale halls. Each step sent a single echo down the hall. Following prior instructions, I awkwardly slung the lumpy gym bag over my shoulder and headed up the stairs.

I'd been excited about going to Outdoor School since the trip was announced on the first week of 6th grade. After starting middle school, I was ready for something different. In 5th grade, middle school was always described as a completely different experience, but not much was new. Nothing better. I didn't know anyone in any of my classes. That was the toughest part. But I was confident I would be able to make new friends in Outdoor School. It wasn't mentioned again until October. Others didn't seem to be as interested in the idea as I was. I'd overhear boasts from self-described "Outdoor School Veterans" who had already made the trip twice with their previous school. I heard complaints from some about how "it wasn't fair they only got to, like, go for three days, but in, um, past years they got to stay for, like, a week," but I didn't care; this was going to be the thing that was different, and I was ready.

It was easy to find my class. Not that I knew where it was already, but I could tell from across the hall by the cloud of kids standing outside the door. In Sellwood the 6th grade had three "block classes," a combination of writing, English, and social studies taught by the same teacher. Each block class was sent to a different camp for Outdoor School. Mine was set to go to camp "Arrah Wanna." We all heard it, but nobody dared to mention that it rhymed with marijuana. Arriving at the classroom door, I could see a couple of other students had arrived already. I picked an empty seat in the back, and dropped my bag on the ground. *This is going to be a long day,* I thought to myself.

## Shoutout to Us

Gabriela Diaz
PARKROSE HIGH SCHOOL
WITS WRITER: JAMIE HOUGHTON

Here's to the people like me
To the hard workers
The go-getters
And the outgoing ones

Here's to the quiet ones with whispers for voices
And to the ones who give those whispers an amp of volume

Here's to all
To all like you
Here's to you
To me
Him
Her
They
And to them

Here's to us
To the overachievers who go above and beyond the call of duty, always
To the underachievers who do it just to get it done
A special shoutout to the people who work, in their families, so others don't have to

To the people who are selfless and to the people who are selfish
Funny how those two words are alike but not, at the same time, isn't it?

Here's to that
Here's to it all
And here's to us
'Cause there is no one quite like...us

## Inner Demons

Victoria Nguyen
FRANKLIN HIGH SCHOOL
WITS WRITER: LESLEE CHAN

I once saw this little girl... When I first met her, she was crying, starving, small, and frail. She seemed about my age, about seven at the time. I don't remember much about our meeting, but then she disappeared.

The next time I saw her again was in sixth grade. She seemed healthier this time; I wondered what happened to her. Was she okay now? The next year I saw her frequently, but I realized I never knew her name. Never said "Hi" to her. Before I got the chance to, she seemed to have moved away again.

I kind of forgot about her until freshman year. I almost didn't recognize her. She was tall, healthy, and beautiful. I was kind of intimidated to talk to her, but then she finally saw me. It was when she locked eye contact and smiled at me with a haunting smirk that I realized I knew her. I knew everything about her. How she recovered from starvation. What fed her? *Insecurities did. Lies did. Hatred did. They raised her. They loved her.* She seemed to have known me, too. And we became best friends, always together, never separated.

She was soon all I knew; she became my world. I relied on her more than anyone, for once someone had made me feel secure. She needed me just as much as I needed her. I provided her with the glory of high praises and she provided me with drugs to tend my open wounds. Our relationship was wonderful.

It seemed though, day by day, as she grew to be prettier and more confident, I became smaller and shriveled.

And so I asked her, "How did you grow to be so tall?"

She told me, *Withdrawal. Isolation. Suicidal thoughts. They've taken me in. They've embraced me. They've loved me.*

I too wanted to be loved. And so, I listened to her and I trusted her. She was always behind me, telling what to do. I grew annoyed but also dependent of her. Our connection had taken a rift. I started to think as my own person and that seemed to have made her mad. She grew possessive, even over my thoughts.

It wasn't until one day, when I was once again skipping dinner and sitting in my room alone crying, she came and hugged me. It was the tightest, warmest, and most suffocating hug she ever gave me. I woke up that night and she was gone. I looked for her everywhere until I finally spotted the mirror. I finally saw. I finally realized. She only left me, the moment I finally turned into her. Crying, starving, small and frail.

To that little girl I once knew...

I thought you'd be my remedy, but you were actually the *poison*.

## Assorted Flashes

Tucker Hoffman
CLEVELAND HIGH SCHOOL
WITS WRITER: COOPER LEE BOMBARDIER

I don't have a very good memory for places. I do however have a memory for emotion. Flashes of light and heat. A feeling of belonging and caring. When I think of a house I've only been told of, I feel warm. I hear something sizzling in a pan. Lunch. Steam rises from the pan and gets sucked through the hood fan, straight out the roof. My mother stands in front of the stove, making something just for me. My mom lives in Woodstock.

My dad basically built the house we live in now. If I think back to when it was being built I can remember a bit more. I can see a long trailer parked in our soon-to-be backyard. There is a small couch inside. The same couch where I first heard my parents were getting divorced. Of course I didn't understand then what I do now.

"We will always love you, we just don't love each other anymore."

I never really liked that trailer. The most vivid memory I have of that time is trying to make my dad drink sawdust. I told him it was coffee. He never fell for it. I'll get him someday.

## Be Better

Iris Campbell
GRANT HIGH SCHOOL
WITS WRITER: MARK POMEROY

Ambition is not a dirty word
I thought it had a sort of a beautiful shine to it
Something hopeful, promising even

They didn't see it that way

I saw ambition as religion
The thing that kept me breathing
I was a disoriented, broken little thing
My ambitions were all I had

I was fourteen, a sophomore too young for the grade
I was full of righteous pain and pious fury
I sobbed so hard it hurt when I got a C in math

And yet all they saw was some high-strung little brat
And then they accused: "You think you're better than us!"

"But no! No!"
I wasn't *better*
*It was ambition*

They rolled their eyes when
I cursed alcohol for evil
Shied away from weed,
Denounced pills as devilry

So I had no fun, huh?
I was a bore
*Uptight*, worst of all

But when one big sister is an agoraphobic alcoholic,

One a recovering heroin addict, still vampire-pale and stick-skinny
When alcoholism, addiction, violence flowed through
My bloodline like sewage

How could I not fear intoxicants?
How could I not equate drunkenness with failure?
How could I not see weed as the path straight to addiction?

I was a jittery mess of emotions and anxiety
Twitchy with fear and pain
My heart even worse

And of course I've changed
Booze doesn't make you evil,
Drinking...relaxed that assumption
Weed isn't the gateway I thought it was
Smoking a little probably had something to do with that

But the *pain* is still there
The gnawing need to be better
The constant, ever-present anxiety that buzzes around my brain
And the newest amigo, the bottomless depression
And maybe ambition is a coping mechanism

Maybe it's unhealthy
My parents didn't put the "Be better!" mentality into my head
I did
My sisters didn't beg me to "Be better!" than them
I did

So when they scorned me
It felt like knives
When they laughed at me
Gossiped about me
Decided I was an annoyance
Because I had *ambition*

Well, I decided "Fuck that!"
And off I went, and never looked back

# The Man with the Camera

Maddie Hines
WILSON HIGH SCHOOL
WITS WRITER: LISA EISENBERG

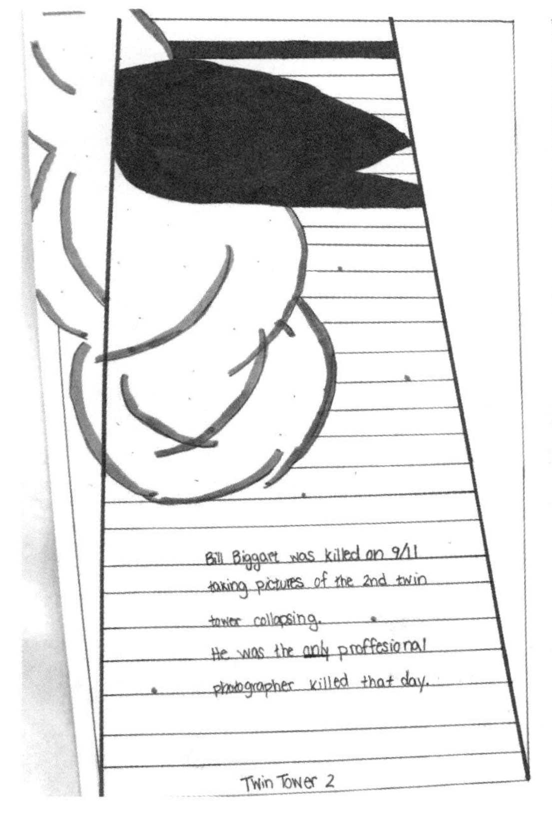

Bill Biggart was killed on 9/11 taking pictures of the 2nd twin tower collapsing.
He was the only proffesional photographer killed that day.
Twin Tower 2


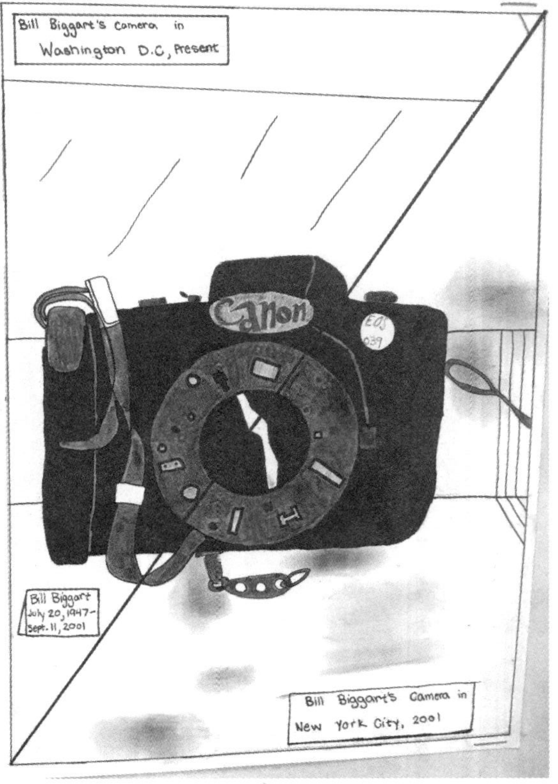

Bill Biggart's Camera in Washington D.C, Present
Canon
EOS 039
Bill Biggart July 20, 1947– Sept. 11, 2001
Bill Biggart's Camera in New York City, 2001

# Ode

Tucker Ensminger
ROOSEVELT HIGH SCHOOL
WITS WRITER: JOANNA ROSE

You are long curly hair
No earrings, no necklace, no rings
How come?
You are romance novels and movies
You are pasta with a side salad and garlic bread
And ice cream—mostly vanilla bean and chocolate peanut butter
How about Rocky Road?
You're an accountant because you enjoy working with numbers
I do too.
You are odorless deodorant
And mint-scented shampoo
The same shampoo that I use
You are a butterfly ankle tattoo
A vine-with-thorns tattoo on your right wrist
        A sun tattoo on your upper back
I sometimes look at your tattoos
        I wonder if I'll ever get tattoos.

# Aftermath

Anthony Brown
BENSON HIGH SCHOOL
WITS WRITER: KATHLEEN LANE

I wake up with my head pounding. "Wow they must've got me good," I whisper to myself. "Hello? Is anybody there?" I shout loud as I can. "Help! Help! Help!"

No response.

It's hard to think I'm the only one here; there should at least be one person guarding me. They took everything I had—my wallet, keys, phone—and left me in a dark room. The room feels big and whenever I shout I can hear myself shouting back to me. All I know is I'm chained up on a cement floor with nowhere to go. Why didn't I just leave when I had the chance? Huh?

I start to hear footsteps. "Who's there?" I say so mighty.

No response.

I start to hear more footsteps and engines running. I am almost about to plan my escape when suddenly the...

Earlier That Day:

"Good job little brother."

"No problem."

Me and my brother Marcus just pulled the biggest heist since the Armenian twins had stolen Pharaoh Kuzon's Staff of Gazon and Gems of Nemar. Marcus and I have been in the game of organized crime since before our parents birthed us. Our parents were the greatest heisters in the world; everyone considered them to be the king and queen. Unfortunately, ten years ago they went on a mission with their great friends the Armenian parents. They were on their way to steal their rival's whole life's net worth in New Panama City.

When our parents and the Armenians got to their rival's hideout they found out it was a trap. Hit with supposedly a beam that was to disintegrate the rival's inventions never really worked. The rivals caused a massive earthquake across the whole city of New Panama, covering it in rocks and filling it with ashes. That was the last day we heard from them.

"Lil' bro, what's wrong?"

"It's just pulling off big scores like this reminds me of Mom and Dad."

"I know, bro, I miss them too."

We finally made it to the hideout filled with gems, relics, priceless paintings, and ancient artifacts. We sat on our gold-plated couch counting our earnings, and man were there a lot of zeros. We ended up with over $900 billion each.

"What are you going to do with all this cash?"

"Don't worry, lil' bro, I'm not gonna blow through it."

Marcus has bad history when it comes to dealing with cash. Just last month he bought three remote islands and gambled about just for the fun of it. He keeps telling me he's gonna get help. I hope he does. I stay around sometimes to help him manage his money but he needs to start doing better.

"Where you 'bout to go, lil bro?"

"School, where you should be at," I said to him with a grin on my face.

"No thanks, I'm good on that one. Imma go out to Vegas for a while. Call me if you need anything."

"Yup, Mark, I'll meet you there after school. Lay low brother."

"Mr. Rider...Mr. Rider...Wake up!"

"Huh?"

Mr. Darius was leaning over me with a detention slip. "No sleeping in my class," he said, then gave me a big lecture about why you shouldn't sleep in class and how much you miss.

It's not like I need to pay attention: I've done all my homework and projects for this entire school year.

"Hey, what's going on Rider?"

"Nothing much. Mr. Darius gave me detention, but Jake, guess what?"

"What man?" Jake looked puzzled.

"BANG! Check it out, me and Mark just hit the Russian mafia's place yesterday."

"Nice. No wonder you were tired, that must've been a hard one." Jake didn't seem too happy but that's because my brother and his brother Marcel are rivals. Us taking on the Russian meant that we pulled off something the Armenian twins couldn't do. Even though our brothers made what we do a competition, me and Jake do it for the rush and to show our smarts.

"What's the move after school, Rider?" Jake asked.

"After detention Imma fly my jet to Vegas to go meet up with Marcus. You want to come?"

"Of course! I'd never pass up a chance to go to Vegas." Jake was so ready to go. "I'll see you after detention."

Detention here isn't what you think; we don't just sit in a room for thirty to forty minutes, sitting so silent you could hear the grass dancing back and forth. No, instead Mr. Darius would have us doing exercises he trained soldiers with. Sometimes I wonder why he chose to work at a high school as a history teacher and not Physical Ed.

"Faster!" Mr. Darius shouted. "No walking! That's it, Mr. Rider, faster!"

I was running so fast Mr. Darius finally shut up. Everyone was speechless; they never seen anyone run this fast. "He's faster than a cheetah," they said with shock, their mouths open wide.

It's been about two hours and I started feeling my body getting ready to sleep but Mr. Darius finally said, "You can go now, good job all of you."

"Damn, man, what took so long?" Jake said with a nervous look on his face.

"I told you I was going to be in detention," I said, confused.

"Oh yeah, come on, let's go to Vegas now," he said, full of excitement.

Jake drove his car so we could go get on my jet. Jake has a SP Arya, the newest project for Ferrari's Special Projects division. It's a 599 GTO, taking the running gear and exhaust to the next level. The second-fastest car in the world was in the hands of a seventeen-year-old. It only took us five minutes to reach the airport.

I was about to call my brother but he called me first. "Meet me on top of the Stratosphere," he said.

"Alright we're on our way," I told him.

"We?" he said, vaguely confused.

"Me and Jake."

"The Armenian?"

"Yeah."

"You stay safe, you know his brother is kind of fishy."

"Yeah but that doesn't mean he is," I told him.

"Alright," he said sarcastically.

"Everything cool man?" Jake asked.

"Yeah, man, he told me where to link up at," I told him.

"Now approaching Las Vegas," the jet said.

Vegas is looking more fantastic than the last time I was here. The city's shining brighter than the evening star. Me and Jake took pictures with a couple models at the Las Vegas sign.

"Come on, we got to meet up with Marcus," Jake reminded me.

I could see Mark standing at the bar drinking everything. He started mixing light and dark drinks together. He was looking so down, he must've done something bad.

"What happen...who we gotta fight?" I said in a joking way.

"I messed up lil' bro, I messed up real bad," he said.

I was going to tell him it's going to be alright but before I could say the word... *BOOM!* The building was coming down, everyone scattering like little ants running from water.

"Marcus!" I shouted but he didn't respond. The lights cut out, everything was dark, you couldn't see but you could hear everyone, the cries and screams like wild banshees.

"Help," someone said faintly. I went to help but as soon as I went over to the faint voice, *BANG!* I was hit upside the head, not enough to knock me out. I started to fight back. I couldn't tell how many people there were but no matter how many of them there were I was still going to fight.

Just when I thought I was done fighting I could swear I heard my brother say, "Help me."

"Mark is that you?"

"Help me."

*BANG!*

Well, that's how I ended up here chained up in what might be a garage. I wonder if Jake got out, everything happened so fast, or if Mark is even alive.

"We'll if it isn't the kids," a familiar voice said.

The light cut on and you'd never guess who did this to me. It was my brother Marcus and Jake's brother Marcel. I didn't notice at the time but Jake was chained up about two feet next to me. He was still unconscious which is probably why I didn't hear him at all.

"Why would you? You're all I got."

Marcus didn't know what to say and that hurt. My brother turned on me, had me at gunpoint and couldn't give me an answer.

"Shoot him," Marcel shouted. "You should've killed him at the Stratosphere."

I turned my face, looked at him and waited for him to do it. He looked like he was going to crack.

*BANG!* The gun went off but who'd it hit? I'm still here. The gun didn't hit me. Marcus shot Marcel in the shoulder. Marcus didn't want him dead. He told me to get Jake and go.

I carried Jake's heavy ass onto the jet. He was beaten up pretty badly.

When we took off I saw a huge light flash where my brother was and then *BOOM!* The whole building went up in flames and everything within a five-block radius. Marcel and Marcus were gone. I wish I knew why he flipped on me.

"Imma miss you Marcus."

## There She's Sent

Isabel Cochran
ALLIANCE HIGH SCHOOL AT MEEK
WITS WRITER: LAURA MOULTON

Sometimes she thinks about it all. All the pain, sorrow...everything. She hated her life; she hated herself.

Luna's past was a whirlwind of shit she was never meant to deal with. All of her memories were at the mercy of her Creator. And for what? For their entertainment? For them to feel better about themselves?

Her Creator was female, with a round face covered in pimples, small. Her hair was naturally brown at the roots and blonde everywhere else. She often wore jeans and gray shoes with a weird blue and green sole. She also often wore T-shirts, one of which read, "Books are like knowledge tacos."

Luna's Creator was as described, and you know what else? Luna didn't used to have the past she currently has. She didn't even originally go by "Luna."

First, she was simply named "Phoenix." Someone who worked with a group of misfit superheroes. These...kids would have some powers that were kinda weird.

Second, she went by "Moonpetal," a name that was supposed to reference her home's culture with names.

Third, she went by "Lunaria May," and this name meant the start of her real history, and what she looked like.

Finally, her name became "Lunaria Song," which marked the beginning of her life. Her Creator had taken several years to bring Luna to this point.

When Luna was sent away from her second home, she was supposed to be sent to a random universe. Even her superiors didn't know where she was going. But in a way, her Creator did.

Luna didn't know where she was going to end up, so when she landed in a pile of hardened mud and stone, she was scared. She didn't want to look.

As she lay there, she heard a distant rushing sound she recognized as cars speeding on wet pavement. She heard a loud beeping sound as some air was released. She looked over and saw someone...familiar step out from a blue and white bus that read "TriMet" across the top. This person looked "familiar" for a reason, and Luna knew immediately who it was upon looking into her eyes of blue.

Those eyes belonged to her Creator, the "author" of her story.

## Home Isn't Home Anymore

Gabrielle Talbert
LINCOLN HIGH SCHOOL
WITS WRITER: AMY MINATO

She woke up to the gleaming sun as it warmed the cold room through an open window. It was late; she was the last to wake up and the only one left in the house. She was still fully clothed and groggy, and sleep clung to her body like water. In the kitchen, chairs were scattered hastily around a small wooden table. A broom and dustpan lay in the corner, used to clean up shards of glass. The night before, a hurricane came bursting in through the back door. It was late. It had missed dinner again. It was red in the face and knocked down framed photos, dinner plates and furniture. It hurled words that were just as destructive. Words she hadn't heard for a long time. Words that shouldn't be said in a home.

She sighed and looked around the empty house. When they moved into the new home, they were warm and happy and safe. There had been no hurricanes for a while. Not since they were living on the street or the couch of a friend, vulnerable and fearful. Hurricanes came often then. She thought the new home would protect them. But soon bills came and taxes and expenses. The paycheck wasn't enough. Not nearly enough. More month than money. They were afraid. Soon the hurricane returned again and again with red cheeks and glazed eyes and a defeated spirit.

It was the hurricane that destroyed their home. Their new home, their small home, the first home they could call their own. All it left was an empty house, with walls too thin to keep out the cold.

# I Wonder

Lucretia Connor
CLEVELAND HIGH SCHOOL
WITS WRITER: COOPER LEE BOMBARDIER

I wonder why so much hate fills our communities
I wonder why so many people encourage this hate
I wonder why people support misogynistic, racist, classist, xenophobic, transphobic, homophobic tendencies
I wonder what will happen to my reproductive rights once Pence is in office
I wonder what it is like to be in power all the time
I wonder why people oppress minorities
I wonder why our culture makes it hard for men to express emotion
I wonder why women are called hysterical when they cry or argue but men are called hysterical when they are funny
I wonder why so many women tear down other women
I wonder why people shame others for what they look like
I wonder why students do not support their peers
I wonder why teenagers at my school are being sexualized by their teachers
I wonder what I can do to support people under attack
I wonder why so many people are abused
I wonder what people are thinking when they say demeaning things to another human
I wonder why I hear racial slurs all around me
I wonder why racist, murdering police officers are not imprisoned
I wonder what my community is going to do about the discrimination in our politics
I wonder why people of color are singled out and punished because of the color of their skin
I wonder why women are forced to pay more for the same products as men
I wonder why women are paid 75 cents for every man's dollar
I wonder why feminism is "cringeworthy"

I wonder why 51% of white women who voted, voted for someone who boasts about sexually assaulting women
I wonder why a five-year-old in remission could possibly not be covered by health care for their pre-existing condition
I wonder why people who were killed and walked alongside MLK Jr. are not acknowledged
I wonder why people like Fred Hampton, black activists, who were murdered by the police are forgotten
I wonder why free healthcare is not a human right
I wonder why peoples' rights are being silenced
I wonder how our civilization would be different if we had a president that fought for equal rights
I wonder why we live in a rape culture
I wonder why my school does nothing about the segregation, racial discrimination, hate speech and overall inequality integrated so deeply into my place of education

When I walk into my school I hear racial slurs. I hear young people using "pussy" and "gay" in a derogatory way. I see young women putting down the people they love. I see white boys not acknowledging their white privilege. I smell the putrid stench of hate filling my place of education. I taste the contradiction that teachers lecture us with. The ignorance pours from the pores of our students.

## Sent, Delivered, Received

Savana Michelle
GRESHAM HIGH SCHOOL
WITS WRITER: COURTENAY HAMEISTER

Dear future me,

You're beautiful, regardless of what others say or think.

Right now, your heart is beating, your lungs are pushing air in and out, your eyes are blinking, and *Harry Potter* is relevant.

Right now, your eyes are as green as the grass in a well-deserved summer. The puffiness and redness around them is just the plump, sunburnt people walking around in either swim trunks or a trashy bikini.

Right now, your hair is auburn and beautiful as a recently fallen acorn in autumn. The frizziness at the bottom is the tail of the squirrel, preparing his burrow for the upcoming winter.

Right now, your skin is as beautiful, pale, and white as the freshly fallen Christmas snow. The small red spots are just small holly berries that have been moved by the wind and fallen wreath door decorations.

Right now, your lips are as pink as a newly bloomed tulip or rose. The scratches and cuts are just the natural lines that arise from the spring season bringing worker bees that go from flower to flower, making each one more beautiful and unique as the last.

The blood pulsing your veins is rose red, and the air that fills your lungs is crystal clear.

You are more than what you think you may be, and you are not defined by your weight, height, age, number of scars, pimples, stretch marks, or split ends. They are all numbers and you are not a number.

You are the grass in summer, the acorns in the fall, the snow in the winter, and the flowers in the spring.

You are a HUMAN.

And NO human is perfect.

Love,

Your past self

Dear past me,

So much has changed since we've last spoken.

My hair went from long and elegant to short and layered.

My skin went from snow white to a lighter oak color.

My eyes stayed green, but they've become brighter somehow.

My lips have stayed the same, too, but nothing bad about myself has slipped out.

I know we were in the roughest patch of our life: You wanted to kill yourself. You knew no one loved you. You knew you'd never be at home because you moved so far away from the place you left your heart. You moved from Golden State to Beaver State with no true goodbye. You hated every minute of it. You hated yourself for being you, but after all that, you made the decision to keep going. I'm not sure why anymore, as I have forgotten why I was having a depressive episode that night. You wrote me that letter in hopes that it would somehow help your predicament.

And you were right. It did.

However, you started not caring. You didn't care about what other people thought. You didn't care about people's feelings. You didn't give a damn about anything anymore. All you knew and had was anxiety and anorexia to get you through whatever you were going through. You didn't fit your clothes and you were scared to leave your room. You needed help and you didn't get any. You were seconds away from dying, and only then did you decide to get help.

Since then, our life has been on the first upswing it's ever been on.

My boyfriend wants to spend the rest of our lives together, and my best friend, although 400 miles away, still wants to be there for me. We just needed time.

It sounds conceited, but I'm so proud of myself.

We did it. We're happy now.

Love,

Your future self

## Societal Souls

Sam Blaylock
PARKROSE HIGH SCHOOL
WITS WRITER: JAMIE HOUGHTON

Dehumanizing the human race
Human element long missing
People feel the need to label people
One is not a cannabis-infused drink
Needing to be labeled

Why not let these beautiful souls
Spread their wings
And splash their colors

The beautiful
Misunderstood souls
Labeled
Labeled to be in a box
Not being able to do what they want

The misunderstood souls
That want to fit in
But can't due to the sad crime of the judgmental lies
Liking the same but opposing elements
Labels can be helpful and were supposed to make things easier
Not destroy the souls of many
A disconnection from reality opens the eye that no one knows of
A disconnection from humanity causes lives to be beaten
Souls to suffer
In a room of judgment

They see wrong when there is no wrong
They destroy souls who have potential enough to
Redesign the meaning of life

Those who are too afraid of what is right because it is new and different
Those who would kill just because they don't want to change

Then there are those who fight
Fight for the humanity
Fight to destroy society's norms

Because guess f****** what?
At home alone we are all the same but the minute we walk outside
We must be a fake reality as if we had just switched on a virtual reality
A reality that isn't reality
A reality that is all lies
A reality that kills
A reality that causes generations of depression
But they don't and won't understand
And that is why I still fight
'Til this day...
Fight for those that can't love due to this sad reality
But their souls screeching to love but society says no
But they are only bones at the end of the day
Aren't we all?
Aren't we all just humans
Why must that be so hard to see
Nobody has the right to invalidate someone if they have never felt that way in their life
Instead of invalidating
Accept for once.

# The Sun and the Stars

Rosie Crawford
LINCOLN HIGH SCHOOL
WITS WRITER: AMY MINATO

His eyes shown like glittering green emeralds in the sunlight that kissed his shaggy brown hair, making the ends shine, and caused him to squint a little when he looked at her.

The afternoon was hot, the kind of hot that makes your nose tingle, and the pavement untouchable without shoes. So hot, it seemed, that everyone in the city that day had wandered their way down to the waterfront to walk along the path or sunbathe in the patches of green between the trees.

Which is why, when they found that bench drenched in the spotlight the sunlight made as it poured onto its raggedy, old seat, it appeared fate was pointing out the one place it had reserved for just the two of them.

As they sat, she wondered if he could see the heat waves that she could feel rising from the dark cloth of her new floral dress. And as he turned to look at her, he wished she would return his gaze, for he knew if he could just get her to look at him, the rest of the world might disappear.

She turned her attention to the river and admired how some bits of the massive blanket of water splashed around in bulky waves, while other whole sections sat still, as if by some miraculous force no tides could ripple their glassy edges.

He smoothed his cargo shorts with the palms of his sweaty hands and sighed, an inaudible sigh only noticeable in the way his chest rose and fell. It occurred to her how the silence that surrounded them had grown quite impossibly loud; had become a barrier from the voices and laughter of the people all around.

The silence on the bench reminded her of that night—the one they spent staring at the stars that had shone in the dark dome of blue that was the sky. That night, the silhouettes of trees in the park behind his house danced above their heads as their branches blew back and forth in the wind.

He had spread an old towel out on the pavement in the miniature basketball court. Just big enough for the two of them, they laid on the towel with shoulders just close enough to touch and tipped their heads back to the midnight sky. Now, only inches of space separated their bodies prevented their shoulders from touching once more, as they had that night.

A gust of wind blew his hair into his eyes. He knew he should say something, they couldn't keeping sitting on that sunny old bench for forever, though he wouldn't have minded if they had. His lips parted to say something, a few words to break the delicate silence that encompassed their fated spot by the river.

"I love you."

Her voice echoed in his mind. She finally spoke the three words, the words he had been scrambling, fighting his mind to allow him to say. Hearing those three little words was like watching a jigsaw puzzle solve itself: all the pieces finding their way to their other half, matching up to make one big, beautiful picture.

He leaned, rested on the wooden back of the bench in satisfaction. His eyes met hers. They were still as bright as the first time he truly saw their sparkle that night in the park.

That night, her eyes had widened in awe at how each star twinkled to its own rhythmic beat. And when he had turned to look over his shoulder, he had watched as her eyes followed the satellite that was streaking across the navy blue sheet above their heads. And when her eyes had grown tired from admiring the bright bits of light that had lit up their special night, she closed them.

"I love you too," he said in reply, the words now able to escape his mind with ease. An overwhelming sense of joy caused his face to erupt into a smile.

She laughed at him, and he joined her. They laughed until their stomachs burned, until their eyes filled with happy tears. Their laughter took him back to the night they spent under the stars, when a kind of peaceful happiness had washed over him.

He had closed his eyes and laid quietly next to her while she slept, had embraced the sound the grass made when it waved in the wind, in harmony with the tree branches that had never stopped dancing the whole night through.

In a state of drowsiness she had wiggled her right hand over to his left and gently intertwined their ring and pinky fingers. He knew then, he'd never look at the stars the same way.

And she, sitting on the park bench next to him, watching their two unbreakable smiles gleaming in the sunlight, felt again what she had that night they first fell in love.

## Travel

Tori Butler
WILSON HIGH SCHOOL
WITS WRITER: BETTINA DE LEÓN BARRERA

My world smells like French fries
Memory is a museum
I remember green
A snail trail through the moss on the back of the rock
I'm not a superhero, but that's what you see in your eyes
They'll attack with red teeth
Action is a deep dark Red.

## This is for You

Kenna Popp
MADISON HIGH SCHOOL
WITS WRITER: JAMIE HOUGHTON

Goodbyes are meant simply for a quiet tomorrow
Where they are spoken, but never leave the lips of the silent speaking man
To say something of complete relevance that only the stranger will understand
Because where's the fun in a reflection?
They always say what you are thinking
You can't run from your shadow it's always attached to your back and you can't shake it off
But someone else's shadow you can always run from
How far you get though depends on how fast your heavy feet carry you
Because goodbyes are simply for a quiet tomorrow.

While hellos are for yesterday's noise
Where you can always have something to fall back on
Where the noise seems to just fade away with the light of day
But the light doesn't actually fade, it just slips below the imaginary point of no return
Yes it actually is imaginary because you can never actually reach it, therefore its intangible
Therefore it's imaginary
Because, hellos are for yesterday's noise.

Never say something that will get lost in the breeze of a familiar uncharted time
Because why waste the breath on something that doesn't even have the power to actually comprehend and understand you?
Where's the fun in speaking and only seeing no lips moving but only sound being heard?
Where's the fun in saying things that you don't have to think about to understand?

Where's the fun in complete comprehension and understanding?
There's no fun in speaking the obvious easily understood truth about everything
Make what you want to speak immortal and short lived all at once
Because never say something that will get lost in the breeze of a familiar uncharted time.

But always say something that is going to be caught in an unfamiliar recognizable hand
For the reason that goodbyes are simply for a quiet tomorrow
Whereas hellos are for yesterday's noise
So just remember never say anything that will get lost in the breeze of a familiar uncharted time.

# Writers in the Schools

Writers-in-Residence 2016-2017

Turiya Autry's work incorporates the arts, pop culture, and history with personal, community, and political struggles. Turiya has provided performances, workshops, panels, and keynotes to over 20 colleges throughout the country, as well as hundreds of community venues. Her poetry collection, *Roots, Reality, & Rhyme*, is a poetic journey that bridges the personal and political, the mythic and the real.

Alex Behr is a writer and teacher who has played in bands for about 25 years. Her work has appeared in *Utne Reader, Propeller, Nailed, Salon*, and *Tin House*. She has performed nationally in the show *Mortified*, and her first short story collection, *Planet Grim*, will be published in 2017. She holds an MFA in creative writing from Portland State University and a certificate in eLearning design and development.

Cooper Lee Bombardier is a writer and visual artist based in Portland, Oregon. His writing has appeared in ten anthologies and many publications; most recently in *The Kenyon Review, MATRIX, CutBank, Nailed Magazine*, and *Original Plumbing.* Cooper's visual art was recently curated in an exhibition called "Intersectionality" at the Museum of Contemporary Art in North Miami. He first taught writing to youth through WritersCorps in San Francisco two decades ago, and currently teaches writing at Portland State University, the University of Portland, and online at LitReactor. Cooper is currently finishing his first book.

Arthur Bradford is an O Henry Award-winning writer, Emmy-nominated filmmaker, and Moth GrandSLAM winner. He is the author of the books *Dogwalker, Benny's Brigade,* and *Turtleface,* a 2016 Oregon Book Award finalist. He directed *How's your News?*, a documentary series for HBO and MTV as well as the film *Six Days to Air*, about the making of South Park, for Comedy Central. He's currently shooting a feature documentary about Matt Stone and Trey Parker, the creators of *South Park* and the musical *The Book of Mormon.*

Leslee Chan earned an MA from Miami University of Ohio, and an MFA in fiction from Florida State University. Born and raised in Eastern Oregon, she now lives in Portland. Chan was a 2016-17 WITS Apprentice.

David Ciminello's fiction has appeared in the Lambda Literary Award-winning anthology *Portland Queer: Tales of the Rose City, The Frozen Moment, Lumina, Underwater New York,* and on Broadcastr. His poetry has appeared in *Poetry Northwest.* He is a proud recipient of a 2013 annual Table 4 Writers Foundation grant. His original screenplay *Bruno* appears on DVD as *The Dress Code.* As a screenwriter he has written for HBO, 20th Century Fox, and Aaron Spelling Productions. David holds a BFA Degree in Acting from The Catholic University of America and an MFA in Fiction from Sarah Lawrence College.

Lisa Eisenberg is a cartoonist and illustrator. Her comics have been published at TheNib.com and in a number of anthologies, including *Papercutter, Love in All Forms: The Big Book of Growing Up Queer,* and *The Strumpet.* Since 2008 she has self-published the print and webcomic series *I Cut My Hair,* a collection of fiction and nonfiction comics. She also works as a teaching artist with Young Audiences, Caldera, and The Right Brain Initiative. Lisa is currently at work on a graphic novel about middle school.

James Gendron is the author of *Weirde Sister, Sexual Boat (Sex Boats)* and the chapbook *Money Poems.* His poetry has appeared in *Tin House,* The PEN Poetry Series, *Fence, The Fanzine,* and *Pinwheel Journal.*

Courtenay Hameister is a columnist, playwright, and screenwriter whose projects include co-writing the web series *The Benefits of Gusbandry* and the satirical stage adaptations *Roadhouse: The Play!* and *Lost Boys: Live!*. She also created the storytelling series True Stories and SEED, and was the host and head writer for the nationally syndicated radio show *Live Wire* for a decade. Her first book, *Okay Fine Whatever: The Year I Went From Being Afraid of Everything to Only Being Afraid of Most Things,* is due in late 2017 from Little, Brown.

Jamie Houghton is a poet and teaching artist. Her poetry can be found at *La Fovea, torches n'pitchforks, qarrtsiluni, Abramelin,* and *Tribe Magazine's* micro publication, *Thief.* She represented Smith College at Poetry Slam College Nationals in 2006, received a Fellowship Residency at Playa

Arts in the fall of 2014, and was honored to be part of Young Audiences Teaching Artist Studio's 2015/16 cohort.

Emiko Jean is a Young Adult author. Her debut novel, *We'll Never Be Apart*, was published by Harcourt in October 2015. She is working on her third novel, a YA Japanese fantasy. She is represented by Erin Harris at Folio Literary Management. When she's not writing, she's reading. She lives in Vancouver, Washington with her husband and very large dog and loves the rain.

Brian Kettler earned his MFA in Playwriting from the University of Texas-Austin, where he studied under Steven Dietz. His full-length plays include *Poor Boys' Chorus* and *Lyla School*, both of which received full productions at UT-Austin. His short play, *Clown Room*, was selected for the 2014 Theater Masters National MFA Playwrights Festival, with productions in Aspen and New York City. This year, Brian was commissioned by Orphic Theater Company to write an original adaptation of Euripides' *Iphigenia Among the Taurians*. In Portland, Brian has worked with the August Wilson Red Door Project, the Right Brain Initiative and PlayWrite, Inc. He is a former recipient of the Oregon Literary Fellowship in Drama.

Ramiza Koya's fiction and nonfiction have appeared in publications such as *Washington Square Review, Lumina,* and *Catamaran,* and she has been a fellow at both MacDowell Colony and Blue Mountain Center. She has both a BA and an MFA from Sarah Lawrence College, and has taught in Spain, the Czech Republic, and Morocco. In addition to teaching composition courses, she also works as a freelance writer and editor.

Kathleen Lane's middle-grade novel, *The Best Worst Thing*, was published by Little, Brown in spring 2016, and she is currently working on a short story collection and young adult novel. She's taught writing as a visiting instructor at Pacific Northwest College of Art, and before Portland co-founded ART 180, a nonprofit in Richmond, Virginia that gives kids living in challenging circumstances the chance to express themselves through art, and to share their stories with the community through readings, performances, exhibits, and public installations. Along with Margaret Malone, she hosts the Portland art and literary event series SHARE.

Bettina de León Barrera is a joyful, bilingual writer born in Los Angeles, California of Guatemalan descent. In addition to being a community activist, she is a Graduate of UC Berkeley and attended graduate studies at St. Mary's College in Moraga and Mills College in Oakland, CA. Her poetry recently appeared in *New American Writing* and was chosen as a finalist for the *Boston Review* 2014 Discovery contest.

Zeloszelos Marchandt is a multi-media creative and arts journalist. Their articles, opinions, photography and illustrations have been published in the *Willamette Week, Portland Mercury, Northwest Kids, Portland Family, Drainage,* and more. They've covered a myriad of music festivals, interdisciplinary events and have directed projects aimed to preserve and project ethnic American history while responding supportively to communities made of different experiences.

Monty Mickelson is the author of the novel *Purgatory* (St. Martin's Press), for which he received a Bush Foundation Individual Artist Fellowship. Mickelson's short fiction has been published in *Loonfeather, Minnesota Monthly*, and *The Whistling Fire*. His creative journalism and essays have been published online at *Gently Read Literature* and Salon. Two of his YA feature film scripts have been produced for cable television. Mickelson has an MFA in Creative Writing and Writing for the Performing Arts from the University of California, Riverside.

Amy Minato is the author of a memoir, *Siesta Lane*, and two poetry collections, *Hermit Thrush* and *The Wider Lens*. Amy has been a recipient of both a Literary Arts Fellowship for her poetry and a Walden Residency for her prose. She teaches writing through Multnomah Art Center, Fishtrap, and at Breitenbush Retreat Center as well as a community service course in sustainable living at Portland State University. She holds both an MFA in Creative Writing and an MS in Environmental Studies from the University of Oregon.

Laura Moulton is the founder of Street Books, a bicycle-powered mobile library that serves people who live outside in Portland, Oregon. She has taught writing in public schools, prisons, and teen shelters, and is an adjunct professor at Marylhurst University and Lewis & Clark College. Her social art practice projects have involved postal workers, immigrants, prisoners and students. She earned an MFA from Eastern Washington University.

Mark Pomeroy is the author of *The Brightwood Stillness.* He has received an Oregon Literary Fellowship for fiction and a residency at Caldera Arts. His short stories, poems, and essays have appeared in *Open Spaces, The Wordstock 10, Portland Magazine, The Oregonian,* and *What Teaching Means: Stories from America's Classrooms.* A former classroom teacher, he holds an MA in English Education from Teachers College, Columbia University, where he was a Fellow in Teaching.

Matthew Robinson is a writer and educator living in Portland, Oregon. He is the author of *The Horse Latitudes* (Propeller Books, 2016) and his words have most recently appeared in *Grist, Clackamas Literary Review, O-Dark-Thirty,* and the war anthology *The Road Ahead* (Pegasus Books, 2017). Matthew earned his MFA in fiction from Portland State University and is the recipient of an Oregon Literary Fellowship for fiction.

Joanna Rose is the author of the award-winning novel *Little Miss Strange* (PNBA Fiction Prize). Other work has appeared in numerous literary journals. Her story "A Good Crack and Break" is in the Forest Avenue Press anthology, *The Rain, and the Night, and the River,* and an essay, "The Thing with Feathers" (Oregon Humanities) was listed as a Notable in *2015 Best American Essays.* She started out with the Dangerous Writers oh so many years ago, and now she and her teaching partner Stevan Allred host the regular Pinewood Table prose critique group.

Stacey Tran is a writer from Portland, OR. She curates Tender Table and her writing can be found in *diaCRITICS, The Fanzine, Gramma,* and *The Volta.* Wendy's Subway released her first chapbook, *Fake Haiku* (February 2017). Tran is a 2017-18 WITS apprentice.

# Index

**Lincoln High School cont.**



**Madison High School**



**Parkrose High School**



**Roosevelt High School**



**Wilson High School**

# Youth Programs Support 2016-17

P.C.Cast

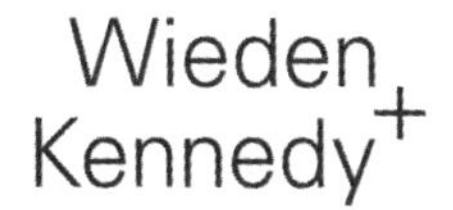

Anonymous

Autzen Foundation

Mike R. Barr

Kim & Daniel Bissell

Bora Architects

Broadway Books

Susan & Michael Burmeister-Brown

Amy Carlsen Kohnstamm & Kevin Kohnstamm

The Collins Foundation

Rick Comandich

Betsy Cramer

Marian Creamer

Catherine Crooker

Marian Davis & Peter Librizzo

Amy Donohue & Paul McKean

Theodore & Nancy Downes-Le Guin

Ann & Mark Edlen Family

Sue & Ed Einowski

Ellen Fader

Jinx Faulkner & Paul Koehler

Caroline Fenn & Mark Bohn

Joan Fondell

Bob Geddes

Sara & Andrew Guest

Susan Hathaway-Marxer & Larry Marxer

The Bill Healy Foundation

Betsy & Tom Henning

Henry L. Hillman, Jr. Foundation

Anne Hoot

Becky Jackson

Susheela Jayapal

Jeff Jones & Donna Wax

KeyBank

Kinder Morgan Foundation

Carol & Max Lyons

Phillip M. Margolin

Carolyn & Larry McKinney

Sally McPherson & Melinda Helms

Richard H. Meeker & Ellen F. Rosenblum

Susan Mersereau

Melissa Mills & Doug Tunnell

Deidra Miner

Jessica Mozeico

Corrine Oishi

Jan & Steve Oliva

Andrew & Veronica Proctor

Amy Prosenjak & Steven Guy

Jon Raymond

Arlene Schnitzer

Rachael Spavins

Storms Family Foundation

Bob Speltz

Donald & Roslyn Sutherland

Herbert A. Templeton Foundation

Trust Management Services, LLC

Debra Turner Hatcher

U.S. Bancorp Foundation

WeMake

Jackie & William Willingham

Tom & Marcia Wood

David & Sharon Wynde

& many more generous donors, including 272 Portland Arts & Lectures subscribers who raised over $20,000 to Send Students to the Schnitz.